"Bob Briner was that rare kind of man who could look into the future and make connections. He could see what was coming, like a great quarterback, and throw the seemingly impossible pass for the last-minute, winning touchdown. His last book, *Final Roar*, is his last pass. Don't miss it."

—**Roberta Green Ahmanson**
Chairman, Pattee Enterprises
Vice President, Fieldstead and Company

"Bob Briner was the best model I've known for the living integration of faith and business. He was able to maintain who he was as a Christian no matter what he was doing. Whether negotiating a contract in a Paris boardroom, hosting a reception in a New York hotel ballroom, or leading a Bible study in his home, Bob was always fully Christian and fully business. His last name captures the message of *Final Roar*: As a 'Briner' he tells us how to be 'salty' to a world that needs preserving."

—**David H. Arnott**
Dallas Baptist University

"Bob Briner's life demonstrated how pure faith and modern living could cohesively join together to form a bountiful, effective, fulfilling mosaic of truth. He was anointed. He was real. He was free. And I was changed as a result."

—**Margaret Becker**
Recording artist

"Bob Briner had truly versatile skills and handled his assignments in the rough-and-tumble world of sports television with real grace. No matter how much pressure he had, his moral compass never wavered. Bob was an inspiration to all of us."

—**Raymond S. Benton**
RSB Enterprises

"Almighty God chose a special vessel named Bob Briner to send a wakeup call to me and so many others. He was like a father to me, gently but boldly guiding me to understanding the hope of my calling and always sowing a word of encouragement and passing along a helpful contact or idea. I hold up my relationship with him and loudly roar, 'Look what I have found! I found Jesus in a man I called Mr. Briner.' Thank you, Lord. I miss him."

—**Robin Blakeley**
Director, Heart of a Champion Foundation

"Bob Briner's *Final Roar* is, as was his life and all his teaching, a strong, clear roar from a lion of the faith who understood the dangers of Christians staying in our 'holy huddle' waiting for Jesus to come back. Bob's passing adds a major attraction to heaven, . . . but his life and his books leave us with a biblical pattern of involvement in the culture. Read this book. But don't stop there. Put it into practice. It's time."

—**Steve Brown**
Reformed Theological Seminary
President, Key Life Ministries

"Bob Briner was a giant among men. Integrity came out of his pores. His challenge to Christians to live out their faith in the everyday world—where they have the most influence—has been a tremendous encouragement to me personally, in our ministries' identical emphasis. His participation in our Laity Lodge Leadership programs gave us all such a boost. Bob's influence lives on, and the truth he spoke will continue to penetrate our spirituality and culture. His books are classics."

—Howard E. Butt Jr.
President, H.E. Butt Foundation
Vice Chairman of the Board, H.E. Butt Grocery Company

"Although the pen of my friend of forty-four years moves no more, the words Bob brought together in his previous seven books were not fiction but depicted what he and other believers attempted to be as salt, light, and yeast in and to their world. May *Final Roar* motivate those of us who state we desire to follow Jesus to duplicate or exceed Bob's commitment in living out the gospel to our world!"

—James Chapman
President, Spring Arbor College

"Bob Briner was so selfless in his giving. If I asked him for his input on something, he would inundate me with information, and at the end of each message he would say, 'No need to respond to this— just know that I'm praying for you and know that I love you.' He was such a precious gift that God gave me. I really hope to be more like him. He so well mirrored what I think Jesus' friendship should be like."

—Stephen Curtis Chapman
Recording artist

"Bob Briner was a friend to everyone he ever met. He was the kind of man who seemed destined to have an impact on our culture and our world, whether it was through his books, or through the cards he would so faithfully send his friends, or just through a casual greeting. He was both inspired and inspiring."

—Chaz Corzine
Co-president, GET Management

"Bob Briner was one of the kindest, most gentle people I have ever known. He was a great listener and always there for his friends. His quiet spirituality spoke volumes. All of us who knew him knew that he cared. I was blessed to have been his friend."

—Frank Craighill
President, Octagon Worldwide Limited

"Bob Briner could, by his example and with his words, reach so many people like me because he had himself lived so fully. And as he lived the examined life, so too did he live the uncompromising

Christian life that he wrote about—one where love proceeds and care follows and generosity abounds."

—Frank Deford
Author, columnist, and broadcast commentator

"What manner of man was Bob Briner? He aspired and did good things for others. Bob and I traveled the world together. We were partners in television together, and partners in the sports management side of our business. Bob had great ability and versatility to excel in the tough world of being a sports agent and sports television producer, and yet to be a Christian leader and an outstanding writer of books. His talent was unlimited, and he performed in both worlds brilliantly. Bob once wrote me, 'You have to be brave enough to live creatively. The creative is the place where no one else has ever been. You have to leave the city of your comfort and go into the wilderness of your intuition. You can't get there by Metro—only by hard work, risking, and by not quite knowing what you're doing. What you'll discover will be wonderful: yourself.' God bless you RAB, and enjoy a good rest in your new home."

—Donald Dell
Executive Chairman & CEO, ProServ, Inc.

"Bob Briner was a person of magnificent integrity. His constant prodding, as my top assistant during the formative years of building our great Louisiana Superdome, gave me the personal courage in a highly charged political atmosphere to take steps that would assure that the selection of architects and engineers would be based strictly on merit rather than political friendships. As a direct result, thirty years later, our superb Superdome is still universally acclaimed as the finest domed stadium in the world, actually in a class by itself. Almost no one knows of Bob's key role during those early days. I'll always remember Bob Briner and his great lesson to me on how to mix courage with integrity."

—David F. Dixon
Chairman/CEO, Dixon & Dixon of Royal
Former chief executive, Louisiana Superdome

"RAB was a dear friend, and it is so hard for me to believe that he is no longer with us. But there is no question that his legacy lives on. His challenge to us all is a challenge I have each day, and that is to be salt and light in this world I live in. I want to be a Roaring Lamb every day of my life. RAB, thank you for giving us *Final Roar.* I love you."

—Dave Dravecky
President, Outreach of Hope
Former San Francisco Giants pitcher

"RAB was and is a huge influence in my life. He hired me for my first job (with ProServ) and then again several years ago when he asked me to be his literary agent. I have known RAB since I was a young kid. My parents were contemporaries of his at Greenville College, where I am also an alumni. He made me his literary agent to negotiate his book deals and to offer advice and counsel on related matters. It seems almost silly that he would ask me, a young lawyer, to help him, a man of such wisdom and stature, with anything. But he was masterful at helping you while making you think you were in fact helping him. I owe him a great deal on a personal and professional level. He was always available to me to sort out career plans and options and never hesitated to use his contacts and influence to help me. I try every day to follow his example in the workplace by communicating well and responding quickly to customers, clients, and friends. I try every day to follow his example on a personal level by putting Christ first, prioritizing time with my family, and helping my friends—or pals, as RAB liked to say—at every opportunity. He hired me to provide guidance, advice, and counsel, but receiving those things from him is what I miss most. On a more humorous note, as many know, RAB was notorious for his use of the fax machine to communicate with others as well as for his odd working hours. My first purchase after becoming his agent was a fax machine. I was constantly filling it up with paper to keep up with the barrage of RAB notes. Fortunately it was a good reliable machine, although it had a rather loud ring. It was not uncommon for RAB to be hard at work communicating via fax between 3 A.M. and 5 A.M., which was when many of his faxes to me arrived. I talked with RAB fairly often but never had the heart to tell him my fax machine was in a cabinet in my bedroom."

—Jeffrey Fink
RAB's attorney and literary agent

"I thank the Lord for Bob Briner. He really encouraged me as a pastor, and he challenged me in my desire and passion to recapture the arts for Jesus in the life and ministry of the church. I thank the Lord for that."

—Steve Flint
Pastor of worship arts, St. Mark's Church

"Bob Briner, CEO, Emmy Award Winner, and friend of many rich and famous, treated me, an unknown new writer, the way he treated everyone, as if they were God's special child. Ever charming and self-deprecating, he'd often sign his notes to me, 'From Your Chubby Pal.' I met Bob through his book, *Roaring Lambs*, which I considered a turning point treatise in my life. I wrote him a fan letter, and he called back. From the beginning he took a mentoring, fatherly role, advising, befriending, praying for me and my family. Though he is absent in the body, I hear the echo of Bob's guiding words in almost every decision I make for my ministry and career. 'Keep a close circle of friends who aren't overly impressed with you, who'll be honest and who'll pray for you.' 'Write to everyone who writes you, return calls as soon as humanly possible.' 'Make sure your business dealings are Christlike, and don't be deceived by those calling themselves Christians who are being unethical in their dealings.' 'Be salt, be light, be you.' I miss The Big Guy."

—Becky Freeman
Author, speaker, and columnist

"The Council for Christian Colleges and Universities has a summer institute of journalism that is a four-week, intensive study for our best young journalists. It's very competitive, and fifteen come each summer to participate in that program. Bob Briner's writings and his presence have had a significant impact on these students over the years. He's still with us, and he will continue to have an impact for many years to come not only in the lives of those who knew him, but in the lives of students who are taught by those who knew him."

—Richard Gathro
Senior Vice President
Council for Christian Colleges and Universities

"When I first met Bob Briner, I knew there was something special about this man. His humility and his servant heart and his profound teaching penetrated my heart. I was convinced and challenged to walk closer to the Lord and to do better things for God. The lesson he left for all of us was to be roaring lambs in the world God has placed us."

—Billy Goodwin
Recording artist

"Bob Briner excelled at living out his faith in his professional life, whether sports, television, or business. Of course he was an influential man in those worlds. But as many know, he also had a tremendous impact on thousands of people within the Christian orbit—not only because of the way he lived, or because of his many popular public speaking engagements, but I think especially because of his constant writing theme—which was that as Christians we should be the very best at what we do and excel in our jobs and our professions by the high level of excellence we bring to what we do. Bob wasn't impressed with his own success or intimidated by other highly successful people. He absolutely loved hearing the gospel clearly preached, and he always called us to excellence, to roar into action, to throw our heads back, to shake our manes and really to roar for Christ. This roaring lambs message was his great life's message, and he was himself a true roaring lamb. In that regard RAB was our real friend and mentor and the mentor of countless of our friends and colleagues."

—Leonard G. Goss
Editor, Broadman & Holman Publishers

"As an influential force in the world of professional sports, television, and business, Briner intentionally, overtly, and skillfully melded the world of Scripture with the world of daily living, and he did it in a profession that isn't exactly known for its overwhelming acceptance of believers in Jesus. He had an impact on hundreds, if not thousands, of people. He was like a bulldozer driver who cleared a path for people to walk the road of professional excellence and spiritual integrity. Now he's gone, and it's up to the rest of us to keep showing people what Christ looks like in the professional world."

—**Stephen Graves and Thomas Addington**
The Life@Work Journal

"Enormously successful but always modest, tall and strong but deeply gentle, busy but always with time for others, Bob Briner was his own best demonstration of a 'roaring lamb.' I sorely miss his friendship and encouragement, but his life, work, and vision remain an inspiration and challenge."

—**Os Guinness**
Senior Fellow, The Trinity Forum

"God is no respecter of persons, so he gave that job to Bob Briner. Bob was the official lifter-upper of those who respected God, even at their own peril. 'Roaring Lambs' he called them. By including me among them, he unknowingly bestowed upon me my greatest earthly honor to date. In appreciation I could wish him no greater joy than he has right now—the fellowship of the roaringest Lamb of all, the LION OF JUDAH."

—**Johnny Hart**
B.C. and *Wizard of Id*

"*Roaring Lambs* really shaped the way I look at my role as a Christian in life and as a Christian affecting pop culture. I became convinced that God had a calling in my life to be a roaring lamb in mainstream culture. Bob Briner passed on to me, someone who was just beginning her journey, some of the wisdom he had gained over the years living as a roaring lamb. His words and his book and the life he lived affect me on a daily basis."

—**Nikki Hassman**
Recording artist

"Cutting edge? No. Bob Briner was on the bleeding edge when it comes to being pertinent in marketplace application and, at the same time, poignant with biblical truth. Though Bob is dead, he still speaks through his books, which are filled with insightful leadership principles that are not simply theoretical but were beaten out on the anvil of personal experience in his own daily journey of following the world's greatest Leader."

—**O. S. Hawkins**
President, Annuity Board of the SBC

"I'm still broken up. I had lost hope that such men existed. Some men shoot off a rocket of truth just by the way they sign their names. Bob used to sign his letters to me with 'El Blobo.' Every time he did that, it changed my life. So good to think my life could be changed."

—Bill Herring
President Emeritus, Knickerbocker Artists

"Bob Briner was a friend and a fellow disciple of Jesus Christ. Bob had a passion. He believed that Christians largely in our Western culture had abdicated their purpose in shaping culture by being the salt and light that Jesus Christ expects us to be. He felt this to be true of the press, the arts, literature, theater, and all the visual arts. I think of my own personal background, growing up in a kind of atmosphere that emphasized that Christians are to retreat from the world. If we wanted to be holy and get to heaven, the best way to do that was to refuse to be involved with people who didn't know Christ—a sort of monastic holiness. Bob assisted in bringing me out of this, issuing a challenge for all of us to be culture shapers by working with and sharing a vital witness with those who attempt to submerge our society with immoral and irreverent views. His spirit and desire was that Christians be involved in the world. This roaring lamb had a gentle spirit about him. He was so affirming and so encouraging. I thank the Lord for Bob Briner."

—Darold Hill
Pastor, Spring Arbor Free Methodist Church

"It was my priviledge to work for Bob Briner at ProServ Television for ten years. I marvelled at Bob's creative ideas, his pursuit of projects, and his innovative navigation of the difficult and sometimes dark waters of sports media. I observed him as a fair and benevolent boss, a concerned and sensitive family man, and a voice of reason during conflict. Perhaps his greatest strength was in reducing complicated issues to simple bullet points for action. It's not Bob's business "victories" that I remember most, however, but his "defeats." For it was through being turned down by networks, sponsors, and organizations when his light would shine the most. Some of his most effective witnessing and strongest friendships came about with the very people who had turned down his business deals. Only a man whose character was shaped by the "man of sorrows" could shine like Bob at those moments. And he did shine, laying a foundation for us to come along behind him to try again!"

—John Humphrey
Executive Director
VisionQuest Communications Group, Inc.

"We started out with a small idea of what the vision and purpose of the band would be, and *Roaring Lambs* helped complete that vision for us. It really gave us more of an idea what we could and should be doing and how God could work through us in the culture."

—**Jars of Clay, recording artists**
Dan Haseltine, Charlie Lowell, Steve Mason, and Matt Odmark

"Quietly and stealthily he walked among us, making tracks in the culture and then in our little pen of subculture. When fully surrounded by woolly silence, he let out a magnificent roar, full of love and anguish, hope and frustration. The power of his roar startled me out through the gate, and the truth of his roar has kept me out. Second only to the Lion of Judah, Lamb of God, this roaring servant leader changed my world."

—**Nicole Johnson**
Actress and author

"The arts, the media, and the entertainment industry, in all its forms, are the loudest megaphones to speak to our global culture. I can affect them somewhat with my boycott, but I can affect them more powerfully and permanently with my presence—the presence of a lamb, but the internal power and impact of a lion. Bob Briner opened my eyes to this, and challenged me personally to express and live my faith creatively in a way that powerfully, permanently shapes the world."

—**Paul Johnson**
Actor and author

"Bob Briner's *Roaring Lambs* was, to an entire generation of young American Christians, what Mao's Little Red Book was to young Chinese Marxists in the '60s revolution. Tired of living in a culture where Christian ideas were segregated, marginalized, and forced to ride at the back of the cultural bus, Briner was for many the only grownup Christian who had the courage to say that the cultural paradigm of Christian cultural withdrawal constructed by misguided Christians and cheered on by militant secularists was a disaster. He was the quintessential happy warrior who preached righteous subversion with a smile."

—**Mark Joseph**
President, MJM Entertainment Group

"Bob Briner was a wonderful husband and father, a tremendously successful television and sports executive, an admired speaker, and best-selling author. But more than that, Bob exemplified what it truly means to be a servant/leader. His books, in particular *Roaring Lambs* and *The Leadership Lessons of Jesus*, had a profound impact on many, many lives, my own included. Bob had a God-ordained way of humbling and challenging me while still encouraging me to be all that God wants me to be, to make my life count for the kingdom and to be 'salt and light.' Bob's life, work, words, and godly example will indeed live on for generations. He has influenced our whole culture, one person at a time, and I feel very blessed to have known him and to have had him call me a friend for the last five and a half years of his life."

—Neal Joseph
Vice President, Entertainment, Crosswalk.com

"Bob Briner lived his life to be salt and light in a place where few dared have the courage to shine. He was not afraid to let the Spirit of God radiate through as a mentor, encourager, inspirer, role model, and friend. As a Christian working in secular Hollywood, I received great support from Bob, and next to the Bible, all Bob's books have become manuals for my goal to promote Jesus Christ in a positive way to everyone I worked with in the entertainment industry. I was honored to have been included in his *Lambs Among Wolves*, and I was blessed to know him."

—Darlene Koldenhoven
Grammy award-winning vocalist

"Everything he did, every person he met, every appointment I ever scheduled for him with music industry insiders—all of it was laced with one thought: What kingdom work can be done here? That is his lasting legacy. Bob Briner rescued me. He listened to a call from God to write a book and then followed up with a frustrated guy from Nashville. Bob Briner reminded me of my mission as a Christian to be salt and light in a dying world. He forever burned in my mind a concept that the world is decaying and that I should try to assist in preserving it as long as I could. If the word *Christian* means 'little Christ,' then Bob Briner is the definitive Christian. He showed me Christ every day."

—Barry Landis
Vice President/General Manager, Atlantic Records

"In *Final Roar*, Bob Briner sends a much-needed wake up call to the church. This is a must-read for anyone attempting to affect the culture for the cause of Christ Jesus."

—Mark Lusk
Vice President, Christian Marketing and Sales, Atlantic Records

"Modern Christians consume media all the time, but they rarely think about it. They complain and complain about the contents of the media products that they purchase and consume, yet fail to realize that there are positive steps they could take to help change the marketplace. Bob Briner spent the 1990s gently pleading with the faithful in the church that he loved to stop and think about these equations. It mattered, of course, that he knew what he was talking about. But it mattered even more that he genuinely loved people—inside the media and outside—and wanted to help them get their acts together."

—Terry Mattingly
Regent University
Correspondent, Scripps Howard News Service

"Bob Briner's *Final Roar* is a roaring achievement. It outlines the challenges facing us all and more importantly it instructs us how to meet those challenges."

—**Mark H. McCormack**
Chairman & CEO, IMG
Author of *What They Don't Teach You at Harvard Business School*

"Having spent most of my life involved in Christian music, I have from time to time over the years found myself involved in discussions with record companies and artists about crossing over into the mainstream marketplace. We were usually talking about increasing sales and expanding a career. Bob Briner made it clear to me that it should first and foremost be about us as Christians being salt and light to a dying world. Bob wanted all of us as individuals to 'cross over' into mainstream society. He certainly left us all a great example to follow."

—**Norman Miller**
Proper Management

"Big Bob Briner! How I miss this sweet-natured, clear-seeing prophet and friend. But here's a secret: His prophecies, his summonses to Christian service and action remain with us, in print as in memory—as vital and as compelling as the big guy himself."

—**William Murchison**
Creators Syndicate

"Bob is a gadfly—but one with tremendous grace—who prods the church along and asks that we take risks, practice excellence and humbly direct praise to God. Bob validated so many things I was taught growing up: not to fear 'the world' but bring something special to it. To use my time and talents to their utmost, and to build relationships with no agenda other than loving God's children. I saw it enacted in my Dad's life, and Bob served to remind me of how extraordinary we can all be when we forget convention and instead work, love, and serve, with graceful abandon."

—**Dave Palmer**
Squint Entertainment

"The Lord Jesus Christ has done such a great work in Bob Briner, and we are all beneficiaries of that great work. When it comes to the theme of roaring lambs, being salt and light in the culture and the community and among our co-workers, no one said it better than Bob. Bob, an older man, encouraged me, a younger man, in the faith and in the work of God's kingdom. Bob never ran out of encouraging words for me. Grace given in a gracious manner through words for the moment—this characterized his life. It was his style to build up. He was not so much interested in the 'score' as he was in the Savior and in people coming to know the Savior. Bob was a magnet. He drew us in with his graciousness, his conviction, his vision, and in so doing he drew us to Jesus, the one he loved so much. He tasted success, and he also tasted the Savior. It's apparent which one satisfied his soul. He was large in love, gracious in spirit, single-minded, gifted, and skilled to accomplish so much for the glory of God. Now he soars ever more. To God be the glory."

—Scott Patty
Pastor, Grace Community Church of Nashville

"Heroes seem to be a thing of the past, something that sits back there in time somewhere, something we've lost a vision for. And when we do have a vision of heroes in our society and in our culture today, it has more to do with the muchness and the many and the more of life—the volume of something, of quantity, and hardly ever about quality. Maybe in Bob Briner there is a hero. Bob was always giving. I want to walk in the ways my 'older brother' set forth for me and in the ways he outlined. And in the same way as Paul had his disciples and they desired to walk in his ways, I was a disciple of Bob Briner, and I still am and intend to be for a long time. I will follow Bob as he follows Christ. In the life of Bob Briner something went very right. This man gave himself away in the name of Jesus Christ. He left us with a wonderful legacy of what it means to be God's man in God's place in God's time. And he also left us with a tremendous charge to live for Christ in the everywhere and the everything of life. God is good in many ways. He is good also because he gave us Bob."

—Charlie Peacock
Recording artist, producer and author

"I knew Bob Briner for more than forty years, and in all that time, I never stopped marveling at his incredible selflessness, generosity, and dedication. There is no greater praise than this: Everyone who knew him well considered him their best friend."

—Edwin Pope
Sports editor, *Miami Herald*

"All of us have heard the quote that goes something like this: 'If I have been able to see farther than other men, it is because I have stood on the shoulders of giants.' Bob Briner was a big man with broad shoulders, and in the last few years a multitude of brothers and sisters stood on his shoulders, and because of Bob we have seen the world more clearly than before. He was brilliant, incisive, prophetic, unnerving at times, unwilling to accept the status quo, practical in his approach to life, gracious to newcomers, impatient with excuse-makers, and eager to see an entire generation of roaring lambs rise up and change the world. Truly, a good man has gone to heaven. He will be greatly missed. He will not be soon forgotten. The impact of his life will be felt for generations to come. Only eternity will reveal the things he accomplished for

God. He was the lamb that roared, and we all heard his voice. He touched the world and made it a better place."

—**Ray Pritchard**
Author and pastor, Calvary Memorial Church

"I have always shared Bob's philosophy and vision that we step out of our comfortable subculture and reach into mainstream America and impact it with our faith. Other than my own father and my pastor, I have never had another man encourage me the way Bob did. He was 100% servant, and I am a better, wiser man because of his impact on my life."

—**Michael W. Smith**
Grammy award-winning recording artist

"There are few 'pals' like Bob Briner. Once he claimed you as his friend, that seemingly became for Bob a lifetime commitment. You couldn't shake loose as Bob's friend. From all parts of the world and at the most unexpected times, Bob's friendship would pop up. When he felt his friends needed him, he was there. Bob cared enough about me that when I fell short of what he thought I should be or do, he let me know in no uncertain terms. Bob valued excellence, and he valued it in all of his friends. He tried his best to get it out of me."

—**Robert "Ish" Smith**
Former President, Greenville College
Past President, International Baseball Association

"Bob Briner was a mentor of mine, and he influenced my life in the tennis world with his advice and counsel when I needed help. His wisdom, understanding, and biblical perspective were always welcome ingredients in enabling me to make the right the decisions. Bob made a decision to change his profession and really to make the rest of his life count most in influencing and challenging thousands of people with his writing."

—**Stan Smith**
Former U.S. Open and Wimbledon Champion

"For twenty-five years as a professional colleague and friend, I watched RAB on a daily basis use his unique gift of distilling very complicated issues down to the most simple basics. He used this gift successfully in coaching, in promoting the Miami Dolphins, in helping the Superdome in New Orleans get built, in creating World Championship Tennis, in running the Association of Tennis Professionals, in creating award-winning television programming for ProServ, and in ministry. To be in the trenches with RAB and to learn from him was as great an experience in life as I could have ever imagined."

—**Dennis Spencer**
SFX Sports Group

"I first met Bob after I read *Roaring Lambs*, and it just resonated within me because my whole life has been dedicated to helping people bring their faith and the culture they live in together somehow, to live an integrated, non-compartmentalized Christian life. Bob emdodied that and preached that. I was struck with how incredibly open and giving he was. I would consider him a personal and business mentor. He was the epitome of professional courtesy and personal humility. What a model of dignity, grace, and style he was. If I could even be a tenth of what this man was in his graciousness, his social skills, his politeness, I would be a better person."

—John W. Styll
President, CCM Communications
Publisher and Executive Editor, *CCM Magazine*

"I can't remember a time when I was first introduced to the man by the writings, and then on meeting the man I felt such complete harmony between what I'd read and who this person was. I think it's fair to say that Bob was Squint's patron saint."

—Steve Taylor
President, Squint Entertainment

"Bob Briner is—not *was,* for God *is* the God of the living—a man who always puts his faith where his mouth is. That's why it sounds so much like a roar in a culture that has grown tone-deaf to the voice of God."

—Cal Thomas
Syndicated columnist

"Several years ago a friend gave me a copy of Bob Briner's *Roaring Lambs*. After reading Bob's words on the biblical principle of being salt and light in our culture, I realized I was essentially spiritually cocooned. Everyone in my life was a Christian. Bob's writings and later his friendship provided a springboard for me to expand my horizons and look beyond my own little world into God's great big universe."

—Dick Tunney
Recording artist

"In my twelve years of service as Mr. Briner's personal assistant, I can sum up in two words the impact he had in my life: *meaning* and *significance*. I feel this is the most important legacy he will leave for all of us. Make sure that everything you say and do has meaning and significance. Make sure everything counts. I feel God placed me in my job so I could have a closer personal relationship with him through my working relationship with Mr. Briner. I honestly feel I wouldn't be steadfast in my love for Christ if it had not been for Mr. Briner, who is an excellent example to me of a businessman, a father, and most importantly a follower of Christ. *Final Roar* is the final impact he will have on all our lives. I want to challenge you to give significance and meaning to your life, to go out there and to be roaring lambs—even if the roar is quiet. I miss you, sir."

—**Mary Ann Van Meter**
Assistant to Bob Briner at ProServ Television, Inc.
VisionQuest Communications Group

"Bob 'RAB' Briner was one of God's great, humble servants. Bob was so close to what I was doing, and when the days were dark and rough, he was there. He had seen the end, and he knew it was going to be all right. Bob's creative mind was always working. It was rich and fertile. God had given him an incredible sense of creativity. He was not just a sports manager; he was a creative person of God. And that creativity showed in everything he did. He helped to create people and their lives, he helped to mold and shape them, and graciously he gave of his own being so that others could succeed. The wolves will not win the battle, because Bob Briner has seen to it that great seeds have been sown, that the harvest is prepared, that the persons who can defeat the wolves are on the march, and that they are being creative in making inroads against the wolves who have controlled our world. How appropriate it is that a person uniquely like Bob Briner could have had a place in this world. We honor Bob by roaring the loudest we have ever roared. His final book is *Final Roar*, but that echo will go on for generations and generations and forever and ever, because Bob was a man who walked only with God and his Savior, Jesus our Lord."

—**Ken Wales**
Executive Producer, *Christy* TV series

"During my entire career at ABC News, Bob Briner reached out to support me through prayer, books, and encouraging calls and notes. His passion and vision for the Christian in the secular marketplace was and continues to be an inspiration in my work as a television journalist."

—**Peggy Wehmeyer**
Correspondent, ABC News

"Bob Briner is a father and mentor to many of us in the arts, media, and entertainment community who have determined to work our craft in the marketplace of ideas beyond the imaginary boundaries of a shallow religious subculture. We are devoted to the work that has been given to us but, as we were well taught by the way in which Bob lived his life, to do so with inimitable kindness and an unswerving commitment to excellence. People, whoever they may be, are more important than our mission. As busy as he was, he always seemed to have time to teach what he had learned and to give what he had received. Bob Briner never misled me, whether it was on the fine points of a deal, who the good guys are, or where to find the best foie gras in Paris."

—**Wes Yoder**
President, The Ambassador Agency

FINAL ROAR

FINAL ROAR

BOB BRINER

❧ Author *of* ROARING LAMBS ❧

BROADMAN
&HOLMAN
PUBLISHERS

Nashville, Tennessee

0–8054–2361–3

Published by Broadman & Holman Publishers,
Nashville, Tennessee

Dewey Decimal Classification: 261
Subject Heading: CHRISTIANITY AND SOCIETY

Scripture quotations are from the Holy Bible, New International
Version, © copyright 1973, 1978, 1984.

Library of Congress Cataloging-in-Publication Data

Briner, Bob, 1935–1999
Final Roar / Bob Briner..
    p. cm.
Includes bibliographical references.
ISBN 0–8054–2361–3
1. Church and the world. 2. Evangelicalism—United States. 3.
Christianity and culture.
    I. Title.

BR115.W6 B72 2000
261'.0973—dc21

00–037919

1 2 3 4 5 04 03 02 01 00

Dedication

This book is dedicated to William E. Bullard, who has never failed America, or me. He has been a friend and a most important mentor for more than thirty years.

795

112403

Contents

Foreword

THERE IT WAS, SITTING QUIETLY, ALL ALONE ON MY desk credenza—a cassette tape which my secretary, Sharon Lundy, promises was not there the day before. I had noticed the cassette earlier in the day, but only in a glancing manner, as my day was filled with meetings and phone calls. The second time I looked, the tape caught my eye. I then noticed the title, "High and Lifted Up," and I flippantly assumed it was one of the many tapes I had produced with the Brooklyn Tabernacle Choir. Their most recent album was actually titled "High and Lifted Up," so I can be excused for assuming this was one of those advance tapes.

Yet on a third look, later in the day, I noticed the tape said "High and Lifted Up by Bob Briner," and the heading said "Gospel Music Association, 1994." This was a speech Bob had delivered to my industry associates more than five years previously. Where had this tape come from? Why was it sitting on my desk? The significance of the tape's appearance will soon become meaningful to you. Just over a week prior to my finding the tape, Bob had died at his home in Greenville, Illinois. His wife Marty and his daughters Lynn and Leigh, along with his son, Rob, were at Bob's side. He struggled and lost a bout with large-cell lymphoma, an especially deadly form of cancer. Bob went through several chemotherapy treatments, and he spent the last day and a half of his life in a coma.

The book you are holding now is Bob's last. He burst onto the scene with his landmark *Roaring Lambs* and then went on to write six other significant works. *Final Roar*, his seventh book, would be his final attempt to shake a sleepy church awake and to offer an apology to the many who are watching the Christian church out in the larger world. If we as a church have not been able to reach you—the world—with the gentle, probing message of Christ, Bob thought, then here is one Christian who is sorry. If your total concept of a Christian life is comprised of blue-haired televangelists or gossiping church members, then here is one Christian who is sorry. If you have not been impacted by the loving, sweet knowledge of a gracious and loving God, then here's someone who offers an apology.

When Bob Briner passed away on June 18, 1999, my life changed. Bob was my mentor, my friend, my defender, and my earthly inspiration. I wasn't alone in that way. I found out that Bob had mentored many people, was a friend to hundreds, defended those he believed in, and inspired thousands.

I still remember the first time I contacted Bob Briner. I had heard of his book *Roaring Lambs* from my friend Dan Johnson, and I knew I simply had to read it immediately. I was struggling with whether I should remain in the

Christian music industry or whether I should try to segue into the mainstream music world that had a significant presence in Nashville. My opinion of the Christian music industry was that it was far more interested in selling records to Christians than it was in venturing into new opportunities out in the world to tell the good news. I rushed out to buy *Roaring Lambs* the very day I heard about it. I thought it might hold some answers for me, and I was not disappointed. It was a book that made so much sense that I couldn't believe someone was just getting around to saying these things in print. It was a quick read, as this book is a quick read, but the effect it has had on my life will be eternal. As I read the pages, I was reminded of the calling on my life as a youngster and that God was continuing to work in me.

I wrote to Bob immediately. I'm just the kind of person who likes to fax authors I enjoy reading. (Try it sometime. The good ones will fax or email you back!) I really was amazed to have a response from Bob within the same day. That completely boggled my mind because the method of operating in the Christian music business has been anything but that thoughtful and professional. Calls and faxes go unanswered for many days (if they're answered at all) because, in my opinion, most of the men and women who run the affairs of Christian music haven't learned the rudiments of proper business techniques. Perhaps it's poor organization, or perhaps it's the crush of millions of people who want to be in the music world, or perhaps it's just plain slothfulness. Whatever. I had convinced myself that I was just assuaging my ego to think I would actually hear back from Bob. But here was a response from a powerful and very busy sports/television producer, a man who knows the top athletes in the world—a response back to me the same day I faxed him!

Obviously, I was impressed. Of course, I sent him another fax to thank him, and he responded again! This time, I began to wonder whether or not this guy actually had a job. No one in the world to which I had become accustomed had treated me that way, let alone a complete stranger. This was someone I had to meet!

I faxed him to say I was going to be in Dallas (the home of Bob's ProServ Television). Not only did I get an immediate response saying he would be available to meet with me, but that he would pick me up at the airport and take me to lunch at a fancy restaurant called The Mansion. I began to wonder, *Who is this man and how does he have so much time for someone whom he has never met? Could he possibly treat everyone else like he treats me?*

As I stepped off the plane, I encountered a gentleman who was extremely courteous and friendly, well dressed, had gray hair, and was . . . well, large. In fact, as I came to find out, Bob referred to himself as "The Tubby Texan." He whisked me off in his Cadillac, and we sat down to a wonderful lunch. I felt like I should maximize the time, so I pulled out my list of thoughts, questions, and observations developed in my reading of his book. One by one, Bob empowered each of my probes, giving me more and more confidence. By the end of our lunch, I knew I had found a soul mate.

That started a very fast friendship, one that was built on mutual respect of and help for each other, although he helped me a great deal more than I ever helped him. I was at a crossroads in my career, thinking that I needed to escape the mind-set of the Christian music industry in order to "roar." Bob helped me see I should use the equity built up over nearly twenty years in the music field and pray that God would show me a path to both leverage my strengths and reach out to new avenues of marketing Christian music for the kingdom's sake.

Now my friend is gone. Our home was awakened with the news early Saturday morning, June 19, 1999, with a phone call from Bob's daughter Lynn.

Just a week earlier, Bob's wife Marty had asked me to help Len Goss, Bob's editor at Nashville's Broadman & Holman Publishers, in seeing that this book would be finished. With Bob gone, it hardly seemed possible. How could we finish the words of the very man who inspired both of us? True, we had spent hundreds of hours talking about his Roaring Lambs philosophy. True, I was one of his very closest confidants in the Christian music industry, a world that quickly embraced Bob's books, but one nonetheless that needed much more instruction. Len had the rough first draft of a few chapters, with notes and outlines for most of the rest. He had some work to do. The biggest hole was the last chapter on music, which was almost completely missing. Good friends like Charlie Peacock, Steve Taylor, Mark Lusk, John Styll, and Rob Simbeck could help us with this chapter if we called on them. But how could we do it? How should it be finished?

As I've said, the interesting thing is that it was the music chapter that was the biggest problem. Bob began the material in the other chapters as he struggled for his life during the winter of 1998–1999. We spent countless hours talking about the music section and his frustration with the lack of music from Christian artists and writers that has cracked popular culture. He talked about his joy with a few positive examples, including Steve Taylor and Squint Entertainment. He talked about his lack of enthusiasm with worship and praise music, which he felt was perhaps a leading factor in why Christians have a lack of interest in building inroads into mainstream music. Yet even though we talked at length about all these things, Bob had not completed this chapter, and Marty's request to help Len finish the book seemed an impossibility.

And then, there it was: Bob's cassette—which I apparently placed on the shelf years ago. (Honestly, my assistant believes the cassette was not there on my desk a day earlier.) I anxiously popped the tape into my cassette deck and began to listen. There it was, as if being spoon-fed to me. These were Bob's own words that could be edited and used as the music chapter, thus finishing the book. Off the tape went to Len Goss.

So now you have it, the last work by Robert A. "RAB" Briner. He is tough on the church and empathetic with non-Christians. During our final conversation, Memorial Day weekend, 1999, I promised Bob I would defend these ideals for the rest of my life. I know many others feel the same. He was the finest man I have ever known.

Barry Landis
Vice President/General Manager
Atlantic Records
Christian Division

Introduction

BOB BRINER EXCELLED AT LIVING OUT HIS FAITH IN HIS professional life, whether sports, television, or business. After working as a high school coach in Kansas and a college sports administrator in Ohio and Michigan, Briner became the promotions executive for the Miami Dolphins football team and a general manager of the Dallas Chaparrals basketball team, which became the San Antonio Spurs. He was, with Jack Kramer and Donald Dell, the founder of the Association of Tennis Professionals. He founded and was the longtime president of ProServe Television (from which he retired in 1996), and was an Emmy award winner for his program *A Hard Road to Glory*, which he produced and wrote with the late tennis star Arthur Ashe. In 1993, his film *Dravecky: A Story of Courage and Grace* was named the evangelical film of the year.

Bob was a graduate of Greenville College, a much sought-after speaker, a regular columnist for the music channel *Crosswalk.com* Web site, and co-host of the syndicated *Roaring Lambs* radio program with Michael W. Smith. He became the first Western sports executive to enter China after the Cultural Revolution and introduced National Basketball Association games to television there. He developed major tennis tournaments not only in this country but in Israel, Iran, Cuba, South Africa, and the Soviet Union.

RAB (for this is what most of his friends called him) was not only a global pioneer in the fields of pro tennis, sports administration and the sports media, but also through his books he was a one-man cultural revolution in the contemporary church. As RAB fought his battle with abdominal cancer (he died June 18, 1999, at the age of 63), he worked with urgency to finish this, his final book. *Final Roar* is a candid critique of the religious establishment and the philosophical follow-up to his best-selling *Roaring Lambs*. His theme there, as here, is that Christians should be the very best at what they do, that we should excel in every way in our jobs and professions, and that we can let people know we are Christians by the high level of excellence we bring to what we do. Briner begins *Final Roar* by saying, "Rarely, if ever, in the annals of human history have so many with so much to give to their society actually given so little and done it so mal-adroitly as have American Christians over the past fifty years. Speaking as only one Christian, I feel the need to apologize." This book presents a sobering message indeed from this conservative churchman.

Final Roar challenges Christians to get out of the sub-culture. Yes, we're good at writing and singing for other Christians, and even at doing business with other Christians. We have our own television programs, many of which aren't worth watching and may even be damaging spiritually to watch. We have our own radio programs, too. We have our own start-to-finish educational institutions and our own newspapers and magazines and book publishing houses. We address ourselves in hundreds of different ways, and this usually is not bad. But we have not addressed our culture, and this is always bad. We have failed to show up in the larger society, and because we are not there with any level of influence, except for a sometimes negative influence, we have left a moral and ethical and spiritual gap in the health of our nation. We have left it exposed and vulnerable to all the ills, without providing a way of escape. Bob has said that "basically, we continue to take the easy way out. You can't offer the gospel to people if you aren't there in the marketplace and if you have never earned the right to talk to them. We have failed to give people the chance to choose good things instead of bad things. We have not offered them the best that we have."

This book challenges readers to offer the world the best that we have. The problem with America is not the unbelieving world, or the secular media, as we so often hear from the undiscerning. The problem with America is *us*—the church. When you put the people of God in this country up against the Scriptures, we're in big trouble. Briner's perspective is that when you compare the American church with the lost world, there virtually is no difference between the two. We are broken in nearly all our human relationships, almost as if we had no faith or theology on which to depend. Therefore, our gospel is canceled by the way we live. Many American Christians do not even know how far we have moved from what we should be. We're like the people in the Book of Malachi, where God says, "I want you to return to me," but then we say, "How is it that we've departed?" Yes, the Christian community is still salt and light to the world, but we are loosing our saltiness, and we are no longer a preserving ingredient in our society. Soon, we will lose our saltiness entirely, and we will not be made salty again. We'll be good for nothing except to be thrown out and trampled.

If Bob Briner is right (and I think he is), the church desperately needs this challenge to get out of our religious ghetto and become more involved in making a positive impact on today's world.

What a wonderful legacy Bob Briner left, and I have every hope that *Final Roar* will continue that legacy and influence American Christians to come to terms with our own failures and turn the tide. It was a great honor knowing and working with RAB, my friend and mentor.

Leonard G. Goss

Senior Acquisitions and Development Editor

Broadman & Holman Publishers, Nashville

CHAPTER 1

We Are the Problem

RARELY, IF EVER, IN THE ANNALS OF HUMAN HISTORY HAVE so many with so much to give to their society actually given so little and done it so maladroitly as have American Christians over the past fifty years. Speaking as only one Christian, I feel the need to apologize. I feel the need to say, "I'm sorry." Perhaps others share this sentiment, but I certainly do not speak for anyone other than myself. I do not offer this book as any sort of group apology, and I do not believe in repentance *en masse*. We are individually responsible and individually rewarded.

I hope that this book will help readers come to a better, clearer understanding of who Christians should have been in our society, should now be, and what they are required to be in the future. I want my readers to know what the true Christian message is and what true Christian methods ought to look like. I trust that by suggesting where we have gone astray, Christians in America will see anew how we should change from this point forward, obediently doing a much better job of what we are called to do by the tenets of our faith and by the One who calls us. I am going to try to do better. I hope others will try as well.

It is important to understand that over the past fifty years American Christians have not only done a very poor job for our country and for contemporaneous Americans, we have also squandered two hundred years of goodwill, understanding, and shared values. During the 1950s, when American Christians began to forget our real motivation and our true message, prescient Christians could see a legacy being lost. By the end of the millennium so much has been lost that even a basic Christian vocabulary, once almost universally understood if not always accepted, now seems like a foreign language to most Americans. There was once an almost total agreement in this country as to what constituted good as opposed to evil. For many modern Americans, the lines between the good and evil have been erased or at least badly blurred. And now, when someone advocates "family values," the question most often asked is "Whose family and whose values?" The point is that today a core of shared values is shared by fewer and fewer.

There was a time in the United States, not very long ago, when the label *Christian* was one of honor and was highly sought. To be called a Christian gentleman, for example, or a Christian teacher, or even a Christian politician was a very positive distinction. This is no longer the case, certainly not in many areas of American society. Strangely, perplexingly, the label "Christian" now often evokes scorn, loathing, and even fear! How bizarre and tragic! While the Bible tells us that Christians are always going to be misunderstood by an unbelieving culture and even hated to some extent, the widespread rapid shift in the way we are perceived in America is nothing short of frightening. And it is mostly our own fault. We have failed to convey who we really are, what we really believe, how we really want to live, and why anyone should want to live next door to us. By not showing up in the larger society and clearing up who we are and hope to be, we have allowed ourselves to be portrayed by unflattering caricatures of ourselves.

I think there is ample evidence to support this, but it came into very sharp focus during the events surrounding the impeachment of President Bill Clinton in 1998 and 1999. During that time, almost daily polls, sometimes several polls the same day, were taken of the American electorate. Now many arguments can be made against the polls, including how the questions were phrased, the size and makeup of the samples, how the results were interpreted, and so on. But regardless of one's opinion about the accuracy of political polls, the fact that they reflected a very divided and confused America is irrefutable. Christians are largely to blame for this. Simply put, over the past five decades, we have not provided sufficient context for most Americans to be able to come to cogent decisions about moral and ethical matters. That many (most?) Americans did not come to any sort of traditional Judeo-Christian conclusion about the Clinton contretemps is really not of primary concern. Rather, it seems to me the main concern is that most reached their conclusions without having had easy, regular access to cogently stated, patiently taught, easily applicable Christian principles relevant to this moral crisis and, not so coincidentally, to all other moral and ethical questions big and small that make up the daily lives of all people.

Christians are not responsible for the choices others make. We are, however, personally and individually responsible when we have not given those within our spheres of influence a clear-cut Christian alternative as they make the important choices in life. How our acquaintances choose or what they choose is not our ultimate concern. Whether or not we have given them the possibility of choosing a truly Christian response is, or should be, of the very deepest concern. This is what Jesus was talking about in the Sermon on the Mount when he said that his followers were to be "the salt of the earth." Of all the ways Christians have failed America, the failure to be a preservative in our society is, perhaps, our biggest and most telling failure. While not a pleasant thing to do, it is important for us to reflect on the consequences of our failure in this area. We see some of the consequences all around us in the broken lives of our fellow Americans and in the breakdown of many of our society's most important institutions. What should be of even more concern to Christians is what Jesus said of those who failed to be obedient in this area. In effect he said that they are worthless to him and should be thrown out and "trampled under foot" (Matt. 5:13). It is obvious that most of us have failed to be obedient in this area and that our country has suffered as a result. I am very sorry about this. We are at grave risk of losing our saltiness, of no longer being a preserving ingredient in the world, and of being considered worthless to the Lord's kingdom we claim to love and serve.

Jesus' admonition to his followers to be salt and light is one of the universal imperatives of Scripture. It is not an imperative that is limited to a special class of believers or to a special time. It has nothing to do with talent, ability, or what Christians refer to as "giftedness." Neither is it an option to be considered. It is a command to be obeyed. It is the responsibility of *every* Christian to make being "salt" a regular, systematic, cogent part of our lives as Christians and to be sure that we offer Christian perspectives, Christian alternatives, and biblical answers to those with whom we have regular contact. To the extent we have not done this, we have failed America.

Again, while we need to work hard to present the "salt" in the most appealing, understandable, and relevant ways, we really do not need to worry about how, or if, the message is accepted. We certainly do not need to keep score. But we do need to be obedient. We definitely must not see those who reject our perspective or the way we see things as enemies. Classifying those who do not agree with us as enemies has been one of our biggest and most destructive failures. (More about this in a later chapter.)

Christians are to offer the peculiar and particular insights of Christianity and the Bible. We are not to sell them, force them, develop power blows to install them, sue to have them enacted, or legislate them into being. We are to *offer* them. The emphasis on the word *offer* is very important. By our lives, by the way we live, we are to demonstrate their appeal, and then we are to offer them as answers to the perennial questions and as solutions to the most stubborn of human problems. When we forget or distort this role, we always fail both our country and God's kingdom.

Of course, in order to be able to make an offer, one must be positioned to do so, to show up at the place in the public square where offers can be made and accepted or rejected. A failure to show up in the larger society with any level of influence (except for a negative influence) is another one of the ways we Christians have most grievously failed America. American society reflects the absence of the Christian option across all its strata. Our failure is reflected not only in our absence from the intellectual arenas in this country, as total and as damaging as that is, but also in our absence from the arts, the major media, from entertainment, and from the business arena. We are also absent in any positive and productive way from the world of politics. This absence is reflected in the loss of a moral agenda and in confusion by average Americans. For the most part, we have either not seen the need or have been unwilling to pay the price to be an influence in the culture, positioned to make regular compelling offers of truth as we see it taught in the Bible and as we see it reflected in the life and person of Jesus Christ. We haven't given our country the opportunity even to reject the truth of Scripture because we have rarely been in the place even to offer it. In this way we have not shown up. We have failed America.

It is important for other Americans to know that there are many, many Christians deeply and energetically involved in all the areas of influence mentioned above. Even though, tragically, many Americans think the term "Christian intellectual" is an oxymoron, there actually are brilliant Christian intellectuals—not nearly enough of them, to be sure, but they are out there along with Christians in every other legitimate area of human endeavor. Our failure is that the vast majority of these Christians operate in the context of the Christian subculture, far away from contact with the vast majority of other Americans out in the general culture. Christians write and publish for other Christians, usually through Christian publishing firms; sing and produce records for other Christians, usually on Christian record labels; and produce and broadcast radio and television programs for other Christians, usually on religious networks and satellite links. They paint and sculpt for other Christians, carry on often brilliant intellectual discourses with other

Christians, operate educational institutions for other Christians, and even produce and distribute a growing number of newspapers—all for other Christians. Many Christians are embarrassed, as I am embarrassed, that more and more businesses are being formed by Christians to do business primarily, if not exclusively, with other Christians! I personally view this as shameful. In the light of the admonition of the Lord Jesus for us to be the "salt of the earth," this behavior is without a rational or spiritual excuse. We have failed and are continuing to fail this great land, and for this I am sorry. In failing to show up with our offer in the places that really count, where the moral, ethical, and spiritual health of our country is concerned, we have left our country exposed and vulnerable to all the ills we now see besetting it. We have not provided a way of escape, even though we profess to know the way.

Most egregiously, we have found it easy, satisfying, and sometimes profitable to blame others for our failures. Even though we have not been visible and effective in the broader society, offering our culture biblical insights and perspectives, we have blamed others when they have adopted non-Christian methods and messages. We have found it so much easier to blame others for moral and spiritual decay than to do the hard work of being there and offering Christian truths. It is one thing to boycott the Disney empire. It is another thing entirely to acknowledge that the extent to which Disney produces and distributes material antithetical to Christian values largely reflects the extent Christians have failed to be a part of Disney and influence its market. If in the early days of Disney, Christians had seen it as strategically important, and as a part of being obedient to the admonition to be "salt," we could now be important players in both the creative and management sides of that company. Producing and distributing morally and spiritually damaging material would never have been an issue. If we had exercised the Christian influence in the entertainment world we should have, the marketplace would not be nearly as profitable for that kind of material. Having failed in both of these areas, we now find it easy to blame Disney.

Disney is only one example. The same truths apply to all other areas of American society that Christians love to blame. But these are really examples of our own failures. These include, but are not limited to, the movies, television, mainstream journalism, the intellectual life, the visual arts, the verbal arts, the educational establishment, and the world of politics. All of these will be discussed in detail in subsequent chapters.

American Christians have become increasingly self-indulgent and self-absorbed, and thus we have increasingly failed in our Christian duty to America. These attitudes are manifest in many ways but are empirically demonstrated in two very telling predispositions.

American Christians are more and more drawn to all kinds of speculation about "end times" prophecy and to overanalyzing the Book of Revelation and trying to match its truths to present-day events in order to predict future events. The other indulgence is the stampede of Christians to all kinds of therapy and to so-called "recovery" endeavors. Both have contributed greatly to our failure to give what we should to America and Americans.

The fascination with popular end-times prophecy has been very damaging to the Christian movement in this country. This is not to say that Christians and others should be ignorant about what the Bible says on the Second Coming of Christ and the end of the age. Certainly, this is a very legitimate area of study for anyone. Christians especially should be knowledgeable in this area and be prepared to explain its basic truths to anyone showing an interest as a way to segue into the more basic and fundamental truths of Scripture and salvation in Christ. When this kind of study becomes an end in itself, however, and is not undertaken as a way to prepare for more effective communication of the gospel to our society, it is counterproductive in the extreme. There are even entire "ministries" devoted to end-times prophecy study and apocalyptic visions. Some of these have radio and/or television components. All have some sort of publishing connection, and all are involved in promoting so-called prophecy conferences. These groups argue in their own way various end-of-the-world scenarios, many falsely presented in the name of Christianity. Tragically, they all siphon off Christian resources, time, and energy.

It is very interesting to note that the biggest current best-sellers among Christian books are all books related to end times themes. Frank Peretti's *This Present Darkness* began this genre among works of fiction, and it has been followed by the hugely successful *Left Behind* series of novels by Tim LaHaye and Jerry Jenkins. As I tell my family, who are big fans of these kinds of stories, their books are fine for occasional recreational reading. But they are not appropriate when read as a part of a total absorption with questionable end-times speculation and poorly argued apocalyptic theories which include constantly attending prophecy conferences and focusing attention and support on the organizations supporting them. Many Christians are caught up in this. At best, this is a huge distraction from the real and primary tasks Christians have been assigned to do. It has almost no discernible positive effect on American society. It does almost nothing to present Christian alternatives for the really pressing and crucial problems facing American families and the country at large.

American Christians enthralled by all this have some-how convinced themselves that in their end-times activi-ties and involvement they are being obedient and righteous. My perspective on this is that they are being disobedient and self-indulgent. To the extent that other Americans even know about all this end-times interest on the part of some Christians, they do not see obedient and observant Christians practicing it. They see only the reli-gious fringe, Jonestown, Waco, miracle-mongers, Scripture-thumpers, and other extreme and cultic mani-festations. An unhealthy interest in popular end-times prophecy is definitely harmful to any effort to present the vital message of the gospel to sophisticated, thinking, and often already skeptical Americans.

In Christian bookstores all across the country, one of the biggest genres of books is what publishing insiders call "recovery." These recovery sections are filled with books, often very big sellers, telling Christians how to deal with the myriad problems that are presumed to be besetting us. A very big part of Christian radio is made up of programs hosted by psychologists, counselors, and other practition-ers who give advice to those who call in. Following receiv-ing on-air advice, callers are often directed to Christian counseling centers in their own locales. The whole Christian recovery industry is a major part of the Christian subculture in America.

More and more churches emphasize recovery-type programs that focus on the problems of individual Christians which, presumably, are too tough for biblical answers, local pastoral counseling, or counseling from older, wiser members of the church, or even the healing, restoring, rehabilitating power of the gospel itself. One has to wonder how the saints of old, who "turned the world upside down," ever muddled through with only faith, the Bible, and the power of an almighty God. How did they build the church of Jesus Christ into the most enduring entity in history, and how did they use the gospel message to change entire societies, without some good books on recovery? One has to wonder whatever became of the concept that Christians are "more than conquerors through him who loved us" (Rom. 8:37). Can we be conquerors and yet spend significant time in counseling and recovery? Are these things compatible?

Certainly, Christians are entitled to and should seek the best professional psychological help when serious counseling is really necessary. At the risk of sounding like the ultimate Neanderthal man, however, I feel that American Christians must get tougher and eschew an attitude of self-indulgent helplessness which sees so many of us running after every new recovery technique and guru. We should find much more of our sufficiency in Christ and the answers to our problems in obedience to Holy Scripture.

The basic problem with both the end-times fascination and the extraordinary perceived need for counseling and the recovery movement is their inward focus. The fundamental focus of Christianity is, or should be, outward—directed not to ourselves but to others. As we have increasingly focused inwardly, we have offered less and less to our country and our fellow citizens, and our society reflects this.

The Clinton impeachment fiasco, from the so-called intellectual elite, to the within-Beltway policy wonks, to the media mavens and, most disturbingly, to the average American, revealed a most fundamental failure by American Christians. Over and over the polls showed that most Americans saw their president, and presumably themselves, as highly compartmentalized. People interviewed in these polls spoke of personal and private sins as being in no way connected to a public life or even to a larger self. In nearly every poll most Americans revealed that financial prosperity was much more important to them than any of the, supposedly, less tangible things such as character, integrity, truthfulness, honor, or concern for other individuals. In other words, it is pretty much all right to be a snake in some private compartment of one's life so long as one produces the material goods in another. Where were American Christians showing that these positions are untenable?

Shelby Steele, one of our most important commentators on the American scene, wrote in the *Wall Street Journal*, "Senator Tom Harkin of Iowa said recently that President Clinton was a 'failed human being but a good president.' This struck me as a near-perfect formulation of a moral idea that blossomed rather notoriously in my baby-boom generation—that political and social virtue is more important than private morality in defining a person's character."

Christianity, of course, teaches just the opposite. A basic tenet of biblical Christianity is that we are completely integrated beings. There are no different selves. We are one single entity, and at our very core are the things about us that really count. They are the very things that a significant majority of Americans discounted so heavily and relegated into insignificance. Financial prosperity trumped richness of spirit every time. This reflects what a poor teaching job we have done, brought about primarily by our absence from our nation's most important "classrooms." We stayed in our subculture, and we didn't show up to exercise any positive influence in our larger culture. We didn't teach. The nation didn't learn much about the faith from us, and it is so much the poorer as a result.

It is important to understand that what Americans said about this president and, by extension, about ourselves, during the impeachment hearings could hardly be imagined fifty years ago. All the Christian moral heritage of the previous years was lost in a mere fifty. Believing Christians are pretty much to blame.

One of the most perplexing aspects of this is the dynamics of the numbers involved. Again, looking at the polling done by two of America's most respected pollsters, George Gallup and George Barna, who both happen to be serious Christians, we are left shocked and saddened. The reason? Both Gallup and Barna reveal an almost unbelievable level of actual Christian belief and possible Christian influence in this country. Though we act as if we were, Christians are in no way a small, insignificant numerical minority in the United States. On the contrary, the polls show that more than 70 percent of Americans believe in the God of the Bible, and an almost equal number believe in the divinity of Christ, that Jesus is God's only Son who is alive and active in the world today. According to both Gallup and Barna, there are even tens of millions who call themselves evangelical Christians (I confess, I am one of these).

In his landmark book, *The Scandal of the Evangelical Mind*, Mark A. Noll addressed the puzzle of the polls.

> The most intriguing results of these surveys for this book is that on any given Sunday in the United States and Canada, a majority of those who attend church hold evangelical beliefs and follow norms of evangelical practice, yet in neither country do these great numbers of practicing evangelicals appear to play a significant role in either nation's intellectual life. What a British Roman Catholic said at mid-century after looking back over more than one hundred years of rapid Catholic growth in Britain may be said equally about evangelicals in North America: "On the one hand there is enormous growth of the Church, and on the other its almost complete lack of influence."[1]

By extension the same can be said of Christians in America—huge numbers, tiny influence.

Why is this the case? Why don't the numbers of Christians in this country translate into a commensurate amount of influence? We have tried to outline some of the more obvious reasons above, and we will explore other areas in depth in subsequent chapters, but the Clinton scandal again gives us an unusual opportunity to gain a better understanding of how Christians have failed America. At a time when many Americans, including those in the news media, were wrestling in an unusual, intense, and focused way with big questions of character, integrity, repentance, forgiveness, and even sin, and for the most part getting it all wrong, Christians virtually were silent about these subjects in the mainstream discourse. This abdication, this not showing up in the culture, would be bad enough, but what we did was even worse. At the very height of the national angst over the big questions sparked by Clinton's bad behavior, there were some highly questionable expressions by Christians that received widespread media coverage. In one, a well-known Christian pastor announced that the anti-Christ was probably alive today and that he was Jewish. This esoteric, arcane, and very easily misunderstood and misconstrued comment left most Americans shaking their heads wondering what it was all about and wondering if this pastor possibly represented the level of thought leadership in the Christian community. It added absolutely nothing to the important debate raging across the country, and to many it made Christians look like laughingstocks. We lost a significant opportunity to teach.

In the second, a Christian magazine publication announced that one of the Teletubbies, the British-created cartoon characters currently big on U.S. children's television, is gay and promotes a homosexual lifestyle among the nation's children. The news media had a field day. Late-night talk-show hosts Jay Leno and David Letterman had a week's worth of jokes handed to them. Once again, Christians were seen as totally out of touch with reality and with nothing cogent and helpful to say about issues with which the nation was dealing.

The third item attributed to Christians that appeared on the wire services during this time of national concern over President Clinton's immoral behavior was even more bizarre and worrisome. It told the story of a "Christian radio talk show host" who raised $16,000 from his listeners to buy O. J. Simpson-related items at auction only to burn them later in a public ceremony. There is certainly some sort of bizarre message somewhere in this, but it is very difficult to find one that is relevant, meaningful, helpful, and Christian.

These three news stories generated by Christians during the nation's heightened concern about moral and ethical values helps to demonstrate why our influence is so minimal even while our numbers are so large. When it really counts, we have not shown up with our best thought leaders to offer our best, most serious Christian thinking. We do not need to support Christians who are unprepared intellectually and who make the best and most effective buffoons and fall guys for the broadcast media. But we do. There are many intellectual and relentlessly equipped Christians who could represent the Christian community. We have the people to do this, and we have a most helpful message to offer. We have just failed to deliver.

One of the most basic and fundamental ways in which Christians have failed America is, perhaps, also the most difficult to understand. If it seems to be sort of "other-worldly," it is, but it also has very significant here-and-now consequences. As C. S. Lewis said, "It is since Christians have largely ceased to think of the other world that they have become so ineffective in this."[2] If at first this seems a little hard to understand, remember that Jesus' own disciples had a very hard time understanding it as well. In fact, they never got it while Jesus was with them. They began to understand this central truth later, when the Holy Spirit illuminated it for them after Pentecost. Only then did they become the powerful forces who brought almost unbelievable change to the ancient world and established the ever-enduring church of Jesus Christ. American Christians have largely forgotten the lesson the disciples finally learned. As a result, we have been largely ineffective and have, in many real ways, failed America.

This most important lesson is summed up in the words of Jesus when he said, "My kingdom is not of this world" (John 18:36). This is the lesson his disciples had such a difficult time grasping, and it is the lesson present-day Christians need to remember daily. When we forget it, and when we operate in ways counter to this lesson, we are never effective for God *or* country.

The entire ministry of Jesus was about advancing the kingdom of God. It began when John the Baptist, the most effective advance man of all time, introduced Jesus by saying "Repent, for the kingdom of heaven is near" (Matt. 3:2). Jesus brought the kingdom, and he taught the kingdom. His favorite teaching method was through his famous and powerful parables. He began almost all of them with the phrase, "The kingdom of God is like . . . ." Over and over in parable after parable he illustrated the reality of this kingdom. Every time his disciples attempted to distract him from teaching about this kingdom, by introducing what they considered to be more practical real-world concerns, he knocked them back.

Where is this kingdom? It is in the heart of every believer, in every heart where Jesus reigns. I know. This sounds sort of fey and ephemeral, not at all what modern, sophisticated, pragmatic Americans need to hear. It is, however, the truth, the most powerful, practical, and pragmatic truth of all time. When Christians have remembered it and acted upon it, positive, palpable, historic, and very real-world things have transpired. When we have forgotten it and have tried to change the world with the ways of the world, we have failed and will always fail.

The importance Jesus gave to the kingdom is powerfully illustrated by what he did during the very limited, very precious days he had with his disciples between his resurrection and ascension. Knowing these would be the last days he would physically be present with them and knowing that the success of the entire enterprise—his birth, ministry, suffering, crucifixion, death, burial and resurrection—would depend on them and their understanding, what did he do? The Scripture says he taught them about the *kingdom*.

Building the kingdom is the job of every Christian today. Jesus left us very clear instructions about how to do this. We neglect them or convolute them at our peril and at the peril of our society. We are to be "salt"—we are to demonstrate the possibility of a kingdom not of this world. We are to proclaim the gospel, that is, to offer the good news of the kingdom to any willing to listen. We are to make disciples, people who will understand and accept the invitation to the kingdom and offer it to others. This shouldn't be too difficult for us to understand, and yet we continue to miss it and act contrary to it again and again. We miss the promise and the power of simple obedience to these simple instructions. We seem to think we know better. We never do.

One simple way to understand the lesson of God's kingdom and to see very clearly how we have failed our world is to understand that the Christian's job is *not* to change society or to "clean up" its institutions. Rather, it is to offer the life-changing, heart-changing power of the gospel. It is the gospel that brings about God's kingdom in the lives of believers as the Lord Jesus begins to rule and reign in our hearts. When this occurs, society and its institutions change, reflecting the new godly focus of believers.

When Christians get it backwards, something we too often do, it never works. When we try to force changes in society through pressure, ridicule, protests, boycotts, political power, judicial activism, and all the other ways of this world, we only bring about the kind of societal failures and moral and ethical uncertainties we see all around us. Make no mistake, we are being disobedient when we do this. We are not following our instructions. We are not building God's kingdom. We are not serving our country or our fellow citizens. We may *feel* righteous, but we are sowing seeds of unrighteousness because we alienate people and drive them further away from the truth of the gospel.

It is important—make that *essential*—to understand that all the problems besetting our society which so sadden and perplex Christians are problems of the heart. They are not institutional problems, structural, programmatic or organizational problems. They flow from individual hearts. Jesus said, "For out of the heart come evil thoughts, murder, adultery, sexual immorality, theft, false testimony, slander" (Matt. 15:19). The only way to attack wickedness successfully is with the power and love of the message of Christ directed at human hearts. This is as true at the end of the millennium as ever. If we try to do it any other way, we will fail America, and we always will.

I hope this book will help many readers understand that what they might have thought was Christian, perhaps because of things perpetuated by certain Christian leaders, actually was in stark contrast to the teachings of Jesus. I hope they will forgive us for failing to freely offer what we have really been given for their consideration. I hope my fellow Christians, even my fellow evangelical Christians, will sense some of the sadness I feel about our failures to be salt and light in our culture, to proclaim the good news of Christ's kingdom, and to make disciples of the Lord Jesus. I hope this sadness will be shared by many others but that this will not produce discouragement and further withdrawal. I hope this book energizes and compels us to enter the greatest of all adventures, the battle for individual human hearts.

CHAPTER 2

Friends and Enemies: Labels and Tags, Winners and Losers

"But I tell you: Love your enemies and pray for those who persecute you, that you may be sons of your Father in heaven."

—Matthew 5:44–45

THE 1999 PRESIDENTIAL PRAYER BREAKFAST, OF ALL events, was the occasion for another debacle for American Christians requiring another apology from sensitive believers. This time, the leader of the so-called Christian Coalition refused to attend the breakfast because Yasir Arafat, the PLO leader, was going to be in attendance.

This is an event where Scripture is read, where sincere prayers for our nation and its leaders are prayed (well, maybe some insincere, showboating prayers are also prayed) and where, often, the gospel is proclaimed. This is the event at which Mother Teresa captured the attention of the world by her courageous appeal to Americans, in the presence of a pro-abortion American president, to outlaw abortion. It is an event that has been a highlight and an encouragement to Christians in this country for more than thirty years. It is one of the last major national events where Scripture is honored and where prayer is seen as something real and efficacious. Yet the leader of the Christian Coalition boycotted it because he didn't like the guest list. Give me a break. For this egregious state of affairs Christians all over the nation need to apologize to our contemporaries for the thoughtlessness of one of our number.

You don't have to be any sort of theologian or Bible student to know that there is nothing at all Christian about this man's action. The fact is that the majority of Americans will see it (and did see it) as just another example of Christian wrongheadedness, bigotry, and insincerity. Unfortunately, to many unknowing Americans, the Christian Coalition represents the church of America and the best thinking of Christians. While nothing could be further from the truth, it is the perception that counts. This boycott may play well with this organization's constituents and help to fill the coffers, but seen in the light of Matthew 5:44–45, it is obvious that it is contrary to very basic biblical teaching. How far short of a Christian standard this kind of behavior is can be seen in the light of the life and ministry of Jesus. Jesus went out of his way to meet with, eat with, teach, and pray for *all* manner of men and women, some at least as odious as Mr. Arafat. Besides this, the Coalition's action is so illogical. It is roughly akin to holding a revival meeting, and then, when unbelievers show up, the very people for whom the event is produced, the organizers boycott it! What kind of nonsense is this?

No one should have to feel the need to apologize for this person's *faux pas*. This is, or should be, his concern. Sincere Christians do feel the need, however, to apologize to other Americans when we allow this kind of behavior to go on uncensored and when we allow such gross misconceptions about the essence of our faith to go uncorrected. When we remain silent, allowing the majority of our fellow citizens to believe we support everything done and said by Christian "leaders," we need to be ashamed. When we remain silent and allow something false to be said or done about Christianity, something that weakens the possibility that other Americans might appropriate its truths with benefit for their own lives, we need to be ashamed.

No one needs to blast the head of this organization. What is needed when one of these shameful distorting events happens, which they do far too often, is for every Christian to feel the need to correct it right where we live. For some this would be with fellow workers, our barber or beauty operator, neighbors, those with whom we share car pools, and so on. For some, a well-thought-out, carefully crafted, biblically sound letter to the editor of one's local paper would be the best and most effective way of apologizing for the outrageous actions of some. For those with the platform, standing, and ability, op-ed pieces in major publications should be the norm. From those with publicity apparatus at their disposal, error-correcting press releases should flow. When bad things are perpetrated under a Christian banner, sincere Christians, Christians unembarrassed by our faith, must step up and step out. Again, it is not necessary to attack the perpetrator, but it is very necessary to attack the errors and the misconceptions. When we fail to do this, we must apologize.

The basic, underlying, perplexing problem with the Christian Coalition leader's action relative to Yasser Arafat is that it demonstrates two of the very biggest failures of American Christians vis-à-vis our fellow citizens: the designation of those with whom we disagree as enemies, and allowing ourselves to be labeled and tagged as something other than simply followers of Christ.

The first, designating those with whom we disagree as enemies, is most harmful and most unchristian. It is also probably the easiest with which to deal. We simply must stop seeing anyone, anytime, anywhere as an enemy. Period. Or, as our British friends would say, "Full stop." Obedient Christians do not have enemies and cannot see anyone else as an enemy. Others may, and very often do, see serious Christians as enemies, but the converse should never be true. We Christians are simply not allowed to have enemies.

I believe the enemies referred to in the fifth chapter of Matthew are not people Christians are to see as enemies but rather those who see Christians as enemies. The command to love them and pray for them is clear and unambiguous. We can hope that many who did attend the Presidential Prayer Breakfast demonstrated love toward Mr. Arafat and prayed for him. I believe they did.

The apostle Paul referred to those who are enemies of the gospel. As we all know, there are those in our society today who are blatant and boastful enemies of the church and the teaching of Christ. But even they should not be regarded as our enemies; after all, they also are people for whom our Lord died, and they need to be presented with the truths of Christianity. And this is true even if they continue to reject and blaspheme the gospel and all the church stands for.

President Richard Nixon had a notorious enemies list. James Carville, President Clinton's belligerent friend, has an enemies list made up of people with whom he disagrees ideologically and against whom he is "going to war." Unfortunately, we Christians have allowed people operating under a Christian banner to portray us as having perhaps the biggest enemies list of all. This is tragic and despicable. Those striving to be obedient, Bible-believing Christians must do all we can to convince our country, and even those who claim to be our enemies and enemies of the gospel, that the very essence of our faith does not allow us to reciprocate an "enemies" attitude. We are to love and do good to those who hate us, bless those who curse us, and pray for those who mistreat us (Luke 6:27–28).

In the powerful parable of the Good Samaritan (Luke 10:2–37), Jesus tried to teach us that all men and women are our neighbors and we have a responsibility to all of them. That responsibility is to love and pray for them. It is never to see them as enemies. Even the pornographer Larry Flynt is not our enemy. Neither are abortion doctors, Disney executives, the producers of NYPD Blue, those who oppose religious prayer in public schools, militant feminists, liberal politicians, or controversial artists such as Serranos and Mapplethorpe. Their actions and utterances may be and usually are reprehensible, but we can never hate them or see them as enemies. That option is not open to us. Contrary to some of the banners waved at the funeral of the young murdered homosexual in Wyoming, God does not hate "fags." By our own actions and utterances, Christians in America must do a much better job of convincing our fellow citizens that we are not crusading haters, and that we will not have a part with those who discredit the gospel of Christ. There is no pleasant way to say this, but, in the final analysis, those who see others they disagree with as enemies are themselves ememies of the church of Christ. We have a long way to go to convice our contemporaries that we are not on the same team as the haters. We must begin now.

There is an organization that has supported and promoted the more than one hundred Christian liberal arts colleges in America for many years. This organization used to be known as the Coalition for Christian Colleges and Universities. Directors of this organization recently felt the need to drop the word "coalition" from its name because too many people were confusing it with the so-called Christian Coalition, an association mentioned earlier in this chapter and one that is embarrassing to the educational group. This is just one example, and a relatively minor one, of the problems of labeling and tagging.

Many Christian believers simply want to offer our country the most possible benefit. Yet they are very concerned their efforts might be damaged by such labels as the Moral Majority, the Religious Right, and "Conservative Christians," along with all the other labels by which average Americans have come to identify all faithful Christians. Those labels are not for the most part positive ones. It doesn't matter that many sincere and faithful Christians in no way consider themselves allied with or even in sympathy with these groups or labels; in the minds of many, we are lumped in with them—first by the media and then by most other Americans. Every time an individual, such as the one who boycotted the Presidential Prayer Breakfast, or the pastor who railed against the Teletubbies, makes a public utterance, good or bad, almost every other Christian is tagged by it and has to live with it.

The damaging problem is that even those few Christians who *are* trying to have an effective presence in society for Christ and who are trying to offer sound biblical truths must first overcome negative feelings generated by some of these organizations and the public positions they take. And they must overcome these feelings before they ever have the possibility of winning a hearing for the message of the gospel. This makes the task doubly difficult. It causes Christians to fail America.

As difficult as the situation is and as far behind as we are in the culture wars, benevolent, well-meaning Christians must begin to work hard to distance ourselves from the labels and tags that do not really represent us and what we really believe. We must do this to have any chance of making the maximum positive impact with the benefits that our true beliefs can offer America and the world. We must begin to ask others more regularly and more persuasively not to judge us or our faith by what someone else does or says, especially when he or she might be operating under some self-appropriated Christian banner. Again, we must do this at every level from our contact with family, friends, neighbors, and co-workers—all the way to the extent of our influence with mass media. No doubt, we are far behind, but we must begin to work at this repair work, this mission to apologize, even though our progress may only be incremental. We owe this to both Christ and country.

As just one example of how this might work, when one minister's conservative organization buys full-page ads in the *New York Times* with six-inch headlines saying, "WE ARE OUTRAGED," we might want to defer. We might want to say, in every venue open to us, that we don't want our fellow Americans seeing Christians primarily as expressing rage. My faith informs me that I should much rather be seen as caring, compassionate, concerned, loving, and giving. I should much rather have my resources and efforts directed toward doing good and providing godly alternative to evil than in expressing rage against some group with whom I disagree. This I believe is much more representative of what Christianity is all about. Of course we must then begin to live out those words in our daily lives.

Serious students of the Bible know that Christians will never win as most count winning. We are not called to win. We are called to be obedient to all Jesus commanded us to do. The admonition to be "salt" in our society is not about reversing the tide of cultural decay. It is about retarding the growth of evil better and preparing people to hear and understand the offers we make of biblical truths. The command to proclaim the gospel is given with the understanding that most with whom we come into contact will refuse to hear and believe. The instruction to make disciples was surely given with the understanding of how difficult it would be. After all, Jesus' own disciples with whom he spent so much concentrated time never "got it" until after he had left them.

Knowing all this, present-day American Christians are still obsessed with winning and losing and particularly with keeping score. These things are not or should not be our concern. Scripture consistently tells us that our concern is not "reaping" but rather is "sowing" in obedience. In the Parable of the Sower (Mark 4:3–20), we learn that the vast majority of the seed we sow will fall without question on unproductive ground. That is not our concern. We need to sow anyway and to be sowers of good seeds.

I am embarrassed to tell other Americans that so much of what we Christians do is about winning and losing and about keeping score, rather than about having any real impact for Christ in the world. There are entire Christian "ministries" that do almost nothing but chart, measure, and count all the bad things occurring in our society. This is then reported, almost with glee it seems. Nude scenes in movies and on television, blasphemous speech, curse words, actions considered to be infringements on our liberties, abortions—everything bad is then reported, mostly to other Christians.

Here is the essence of a typical conversation between a Christian radio host and someone calling in. The host begins by delineating what he or she thinks is the most outrageous anti-Christian action of the government, Hollywood, television, or the mainstream press. The caller then wades in with, "If you think that's bad, let me tell you about this . . . ." And so it goes, with listeners and host trying to top one another with bad things. It is much the same with many of the Christian newspapers around the country. It is the Christian version of the editorial policy of many local television news programs: "If it bleeds, it leads." Our version would seem to be: "If it's bad, we're glad." Even from many pulpits, the bad things of society dominate rather than the good things of the gospel.

All this is as if we needed to be told that our society is less than it should be. It is a gross, corrupt, vile, and violent society with evil triumphing over good at almost every turn. What a surprise! This is not news. It has always been such. Scripture tells us it will always *be* such, and furthermore that it is only when and where Christians do our jobs, the jobs specifically assigned for us to do by the Lord Jesus, that evil will effectively be challenged and overcome. The number of places in our society when and where this is being done are minuscule. In light of the vast numbers of Christians in this country, this is shameful and represents another failure for Christians.

The scorekeepers and disseminators of bad news have somehow convinced themselves and many others that this is a righteous activity. They know that it engenders a sort of macho feeling of accomplishment. They also know it builds audience ratings and revenues. But it does not build God's kingdom, nor does it better America. Rarely does it even bother to propose biblically sound answers to the problems it delineates with such apparent relish. It doesn't tell anything about who Jesus is and why he became human and entered our world. It doesn't make friends of nonbelievers, but builds enmity with them. Most damaging of all, it diverts millions of Christians from the things we are really called to do, which, if we would do them, *would* build a better, more godly America. Secondarily, but still very important, it siphons off millions and millions of dollars from funds that could be used for truly Christian benefits for this country, producing real winners.

We must all—Bible-believing church members, pastors, Christian foundations, Christian-controlled businesses, Christians of high net worth, and sincere rank-and-file members of the body of Christ—wean ourselves away from the seductive call of the scorekeepers that make us feel either a sense of macho engagement or of helpless victimhood. Neither is correct, and neither is biblical or helpful. We must also be sure that we don't help engender this win-at-all-costs kind of attitude with our financial support. There are many theologically sound and solid, authentic Christian ministries in which we can have great confidence and who would be wonderful stewards of our important, hard-earned contributed funds. Why not support them?

Thinking Christians should be quick to voice concern to the leaders of these very worthy ministries we do support when we see them drifting into scorekeeping and the purveying of overly negative news. Chuck Colson's Prison Fellowship and James Dobson's Focus on the Family ministries are both godly works led by two of our greatest evangelical Christian leaders. When Prison Fellowship stays true to its mission statement and when Focus on the Family really does focus on the American Christian family, offering biblically sound solutions to the wide array of problems confronting us, they provide wonderful services which greatly benefit all of America and all Americans. When they drift off into scorekeeping, the purveying of negative news, and the creation of enemies, however, they need to be called to account. The friends and supporters of these ministries are the ones who should be calling them to account for what they do with their donors' resources. Everyone, even our most respected Christian leaders, needs to be accountable. When other Christians do not set the very highest standards for them and call them to live up to those high standards, we fail them and America.

The only enemies obedient Christians are permitted to have are those who see us as enemies, and we are to love and pray for them. The only labels or tags Christians need to have or should have are those that designate us as followers of the Lord Jesus. The others load us up with baggage we don't need and can't use.

Picking winners and losers, keeping score and reveling in bad news are activities that do not help the spiritual growth of individual Christians, do not aid the expansion of God's kingdom, and do not assist the moral development of our country.

CHAPTER 3

Raising the Bar On Christian Higher Education

MORE THAN ANYTHING ELSE DURING HIS EARTHLY ministry, Jesus was called rabbi, or teacher. He was primarily one who taught groups large and small and used powerful parables from nature and human life as illustrative stories to great effect.

His most effective long-range teaching was directed to his disciples and apostles who, once they understood his message, became most effective and powerful teachers themselves. The Bible says that Jesus *spoke* to the masses but that he *taught* his disciples. How effective he was is seen two thousand years later in the enduring spiritual organization he founded, the church. And, of course, he continues to teach us through Holy Scripture and through the illuminating influence of his Holy Spirit. We neglect either at our own peril.

By our Lord's perfect example, and through adherence to Scripture and obedience to the promptings of the Holy Spirit, early Christians led the world into the highest quality of education. From the ancient educational institutions in Italy, France, Germany, and Switzerland, to Oxford and Cambridge universities in England, to Harvard, Yale, and Princeton universities in the United States, Christians founded, led, and were the most effective teachers for institutions of higher education for hundreds of years. And this is true not only in the centers of higher education, for the images of the godly school-master and the elementary schoolmistress are enduring if, unfortunately, fading ones.

I believe the precipitous decline in the quality of American education can be empirically shown to track almost exactly with the decline in Christian influence and positive productive involvement with America's schools. Our failures in American public education have been almost total, and our schools have gone from the world's most admired to some of the least effective in the entire Western hemisphere. We must apologize, and we must begin to do better.

In discussing Christian failure in American education, one hardly knows where to begin. This country's great institutions of higher education have been lost to the Christian movement through a lack of vigilance and shameful compromise (which, tragically, is replicating itself in many of the few remaining quality Christian institutions of higher education). These institutions have been lost to a lack of both intellectual firepower and will in the face of the false promises of the Enlightenment, Freudianism, humanism, relativism, and deconstructionism. And they have been lost due to Christian abdication from the education policy establishment, from the National Education Association and other powerful teacher and library organizations, to the lowering of intellectual standards in our own institutions of higher education, and to a devaluing of Christian intellectuals. We have lost the great schools to the increasing abandonment of public education and to allowing ourselves to be drawn into the ridiculous demagoguery of the prayer in schools controversy. Christians have done little that is right in education in recent years, and the nation is paying a huge price for this.

Perhaps a look at one phenomenon will help us begin to understand what is going on with Christians vis-à-vis education: home schooling. It seems that the biggest educational heroes for Christians are currently the moms and dads who home school their children. Now I realize that people home school their children for very many different reasons, and many have legitimate reasons for doing so and, furthermore, they do it in an exemplary way. As admirable as most of these parents might be, however, it seems odd that they would be the ones singled out for such praise and adoration. This is tantamount to heaping praise on those who would do everything possible to avoid serving in a wide-open missionary field to which they have been given a free pass and an open invitation. Our public schools are calling for—make that begging for—active parental involvement. Even though public school authorities may not always recognize it, Christian parental involvement is the kind most needed.

Although some situations absolutely require home schooling, many do not. Even when it is essential for the health and safety of a child, Christian parents, in order to be faithful, need to stay connected to their local public school system. I have knowledge of a mother who home schools her son but also volunteers to teach art at the local public elementary school. This is a great and wonderful example of faithfulness and obedience. May her tribe increase.

I think the examples of our daughters are worth passing along. Our married daughter Leisha and her husband Kevin have three elementary-age sons. All of them attend their local public school. Leisha volunteers one day each week in each of her boys' classes to stay involved with them and their school. She also serves on the school district's curriculum committee. Perhaps I am most pleased by her participating in Moms in Touch, where weekly she meets with other mothers to pray for their public school students, their teachers and principals. She and her husband also supplement their sons' school and church education with regular readings of C. S. Lewis's children's books and other Christian classics.

Lynn is our younger unmarried daughter, and she could be teaching in one of the many private Christian schools around Dallas, where she lives, but she has chosen instead to teach in one of the most demanding public school systems in the entire state. She wants to bring a Christian witness where it is needed most. Needless to say, their mother and I are very proud of our two daughters. I think every church that begins its own school should have some sort of corresponding outreach and involvement with its local public schools. How can our churches have well-planned, regularly budgeted foreign missionary programs and abandon the public schools, the richest possible, most welcoming, easiest to reach, and most cost-effective mission fields possible?

When we do practice flight and isolation from and abandonment of the public educational institutions, we fail America, and we fail in our Christian duties. The rush to home schooling and the heaping of praise on those who practice it, along with the growing number of church schools and other private Christian schools, certainly produces some positive educational, moral, and spiritual results. Without a corollary commitment to the vast public education system in this country, however, the dangers are very great both for the church and for the nation. In the end the cost may not be worth it.

Caring, obedient Christians must not abandon the public schools of the United States. To the extent we have done this and are continuing to do it, we fail America and we fail the faith. The evidence of the harm this does is ample and clear all around us. Just telling one another over and over how bad and incompetent the schools are, how bad and biased the textbooks are, and how bad the educational establishment is does not mean that we are positively and productively engaged. We must begin to show up to help, at least to offer help, first locally and then nationally.

I mentioned earlier the erstwhile-named Coalition of Christian Colleges and Universities. Most Americans will not even be aware of the more than one hundred mostly small Christian liberal arts colleges that make up its membership. I am a product of one of these colleges. After embarking on a career in professional sports and producing television specials, I have continued to be involved with several of these colleges on many different levels. I am both a fan and a critic, hopefully on the basis of the adage that says, "He has the right to criticize who has the heart to help." I do have the heart to help.

Even though there is an element of isolationism inherent in the whole concept of a Christian college, I believe the concept can be justified, both for the church and for the nation. It can be justified if, and it is a very big "if," the graduates of Christian colleges can go out and make very special, very positive, and very measurable impact on our society by being able to offer distinctively Christian solutions at every level of that society. This certainly includes the leadership level in all sorts of disciplines, professions, and public service. The bar for Christian college graduates must be set very high because the investment in them is very high. A Christian college education is very expensive in very many ways that include, but are not limited to, the actual dollars involved.

When one understands that these colleges graduate more than thirty thousand seniors each year, one can begin to understand the level of their potential effectiveness and influence. Thirty thousand *each year*! This amounts to a not-so-small army of some of the best and the brightest minds of the American churches' young people. They are sent out each year to do battle for "truth, justice, and the American way," after four years of what should be the best education, the best training, and the best motivation the churches' schools can give them.

What happens to this army which grows by thirty thousand recruits each year? What happens in the society into which they are sent? A lot of good things happen. Most of these graduates take up places of attendance, if not active service, in their local churches. Most become arguably successful in their chosen fields or professions, and most become reasonably good citizens.

I am afraid, however, that a careful analysis would probably show that the overall results of this virtual army impacting our society are much less than we would hope they might be. Too much cultural territory is left unconquered and unaffected. This is especially true of almost all areas of business and professional leadership in our country. In the vernacular, the "bang for the buck" does not reverberate as loudly as it should. God's kingdom is not advanced, nor is America offered Christian options the way one would expect with thirty thousand well-trained, highly motivated, carefully selected, really elite soldiers of the cross. What happens to this army that grows by thirty thousand fresh troops every year, and why do they make so little impact?

In many ways, their impact dissipates and fades into the woodwork. Some of the soldiers themselves literally disappear. One of the most telling and frustrating parts of Christian higher education in America is the fact that after a relatively short time many Christian college graduates simply and actually disappear. Try as they might, alumni offices cannot find them. Four or more years invested in friendships and relationships seem to be forgotten and wasted. This is tragic for all concerned—for God's kingdom, for the colleges involved, for the individuals themselves, and for America. Worse, it is a strong indicator of what is going on among American Christians at large because strangely, perversely, Christians seem to have a harder time staying together and staying connected while forming and maintaining productive networks. Other Americans do it better and more productively than do Christians.

There is strength in unity. In unity, God's kingdom moves ahead. In unity, America is better served. There *may* be some excuses for a lack of complete unity among Christians from widely separated theological, liturgical, and ethnic backgrounds. But this would not explain why the alumni of a particular Christian college don't hang in together over the years to form a powerful force for good in the culture. Slovenliness or obtuseness may offer the answer. This is particularly true when an entire office at the college is set up to facilitate holding the alumni together. Something may be missing in the program of the college, in executing the mission of the college, in binding its students together to serve God and country together through the years.

Another way our army of Christian graduates disappears is in becoming indistinguishable from the world around them. They fit so easily into the culture and become so like their surroundings that they virtually become invisible. They blend in so well that no one can see them, that is, no one can tell they are Christians who radically veer off from the secular culture. They have become one with all aspects of the secular culture. I have been in the television business, and I have learned the hard way that, demographically speaking, there is no such thing as a "Christian" television audience. Statistically, Christians watch exactly the same programs as everybody else. There really is no specifically Christian viewing audience. Christians in this country hold few distinctions from the general population. We are invisible.

More importantly and more damagingly, we become invisible in the patterns of our lives. A college education and experience at a Christian institution does not seem to affect this very much. Our rhythms become so in sync with those of the world that no one hears our special beat; we do not dance to the beat of any different drummer. We are so in lockstep with those in the world around us that in spite of a Christian higher education we become invisible. (Perhaps it is because of one.) Far too many of our graduates leave Christian campuses and get so caught up in the little pinched-in, self-absorbed lives of so many other Americans that they are able to offer little or no help to the culture, leaving our world unconquered and unaffected. We have conceded defeat on the battlefield of the culture wars and no longer see any responsibility for winning the culture to Christ.

It is true that most graduates of Christian colleges go out and become members of local churches, but even there the tendency is to become spectator Christians uninvolved in the real cause of Christ. This unfortunately is what happens to the majority of graduates from the more than one hundred Christian colleges in the United States each year. They become invisible, performing disappearing acts that dwarf anything a master illusionist such as David Copperfield might perform.

Really, the only way for these thirty thousand yearly graduates of the Christian colleges not to disappear or concede defeat is for them to become deeply involved in a meaningful cause—to break away from the mundane and the trivial and to venture out into the exhilarating atmosphere of risk. Theodore Roosevelt said it so well almost a hundred years ago: "Far better it is to dare mighty things, to win glorious triumphs, even though checkered by failure, than to take rank with those poor spirits who neither enjoy much or suffer much, because they live in the gray twilight that knows not victory or defeat." He could have said that it is in that gray twilight where many disappear—where many Christians disappear, where many of our thirty thousand yearly Christian college graduates seem to be consumed. No unity, no accountability, no cause, no visibility, no God-honoring kingdom building, and no commitment to offer to our country or even our Christian community what we feel it most needs.

For many reasons our Christian colleges have not been very effective in mobilizing, inspiring, or energizing these wonderful young people in a way to justify the high cost of their education both in terms of dollars and of isolation. All the reasons for this are beyond available space and my ability to deal with here. Much is at stake, and it does warrant scholarly research and a resulting book.

Because I have been spending so much time on both Christian college campuses and on major secular university campuses, I can at least provide some anecdotal and comparative information.

It is important to know that the alliance of Christian colleges is not monolithic but rather represents a very wide variety of institutions of higher education. Really, the only things they have in common are full accreditation and a commitment, as they see it, to the Lord Jesus Christ. What goes on at a Calvin College, one of the largest and most prestigious of the Christian colleges, is vastly different from what goes on at a much smaller Sterling College, out on the plains of Kansas. So, I hope that what I offer will be helpful. While it is from a good deal of personal experience, it is not meant to be exhaustive or inclusive. The observations will be general rather than specific.

Generally speaking, and as you might guess, the lack of productivity of our Christian colleges, particularly as this relates to providing real impact for our nation commensurate with the investment in them, goes back to the homes and churches from which the students came. It relates to vision and leadership, which are often synonymous.

I believe the current prevailing atmosphere at most Christian colleges is a defensive one. Most parents, churches, and supporting denominations send their students to these campuses in hopes of protecting them from the evils of a society they see as completely alien to their values and beliefs. Their highest aspiration for them seems to be to get them back as unscathed as possible, hopefully with a spouse with a similar belief system. There is nothing really wrong with this, except that it ignores the admonition to be "salt" in our world and to obey the command of the Great Commission. There is just far too much fortress mentality and not enough "Onward Christian soldiers marching as to war." As a result, most graduates are neither inspired nor equipped to go out to do the very tough work of influencing the nation with Christian truth-claims. Our country is poorer as a result.

As we have said, the problem doesn't begin on the campuses but in the homes and churches of the students. For the past several years I have been working each semester with twenty student athletes—ten men and ten women on a Christian college campus. For the most part these are senior students who have been on campus for four years. They are wonderful young people, bright and alert. They also have a tremendous interest in the Christian life. As busy as they are as student athletes, they give up a significant amount of time to study the Scriptures with me—for no academic credit. They want to learn. The majority of them come from fine Christian homes, and they have been going to church and Sunday school all their lives. So far, so good. The problem is that almost all of these young adults are basically biblically illiterate. After a lifetime in church and Sunday school and four years on a Christian college campus, just as they are leaving to go to graduate or professional school or into the work force, they are only now beginning any sort of intense study of Christian doctrine. In short, they are ill equipped to serve our country by offering alternative ways of thinking about the major issues of our time. We have not produced very many serious and thoughtful students in the American evangelical movement.

Almost as damaging is a decided lack of sophistication about the ways of the world. In the vernacular, they lack "street smarts." Because of a lack of language skills, basic manners, and knowledge of the arts and current events, these friends will be restricted as to the levels of our society into which they can move and into which they can carry the light of Christian truth. No level of society needs or deserves the chance to choose a biblical way of thinking more than any other. No level deserves it less. Most current Christian college graduates have only minimal possibilities of ever being able to impact the leadership levels, which are, like it or not, the most strategic. As a result, the nation is poorer.

Obviously, what is needed in the Christian college movement, if it is to achieve anywhere near its potential for good and if its very sizable investment is to produce an acceptable return, is a much stronger commitment to service and a much sharper, more focused vision of what that service should be. There must be more than a minimal commitment to serve the community and the nation. It would be most helpful if more Christian homes and churches would step up in better preparing their young people, first for college and then for service, but the colleges can't wait for them. They must take the lead.

The mission statement at my Christian college alma mater says the college exists to produce servant leaders. Some sort of servant-leader language is probably a part of most Christian college mission statements. Finding it much easier to produce servants than it is to produce leaders, however, Christian institutions of higher education pay only lip service to any authentic leadership emphasis. Producing leaders is very expensive, not only in terms of the investment dollars involved, but also in terms of plain hard work. It takes diligence, attention to detail, intellectual rigor, and an unwavering commitment to excellence. It takes the kind of faculty dedication that was once the Christian college norm, but which is now in increasingly short supply. To produce leaders, Christian faculty cannot "mail it in," and academic administrators must recruit professors who understand what this kind of commitment entails and who are dedicated to teaching and mentoring.

Mentoring is a key term. As important as classroom teaching is, and as essential as it is that it be excellent, it can never produce Christian leaders by itself. Students must be mentored, or, to use the biblical term, they must be *discipled*. This requires one-on-one relationships between faculty and students. W. Richard Stephens, a Christian college president himself, has said that the bulk of the Christianizing impact of private colleges occurs not in the chapels but in the extended daily interactions, both in and out of class, between faculty and students. Christian college presidents and chief academic officers must be sure their faculty understand and commit to making disciples of their students outside the classroom. The preparation these students need to better serve America, as well as their faith, can never be facilitated by professors who teach their required academic load only to escape from campus and avoid additional contact.

No apologies should be made in expecting professional educators teaching in a Christian college to commit to outside-of-class mentoring or discipling. The Great Commission commands every Christian to be a discipler. It is not an option for obedient Christians. Of all the people on planet Earth, Christian college faculty should embrace and revel in the built-in opportunity they have to build positive, powerful, personal relationships with their students. This is absolutely necessary if there is to be any chance of producing the Christian servant-leaders our nation needs and deserves.

Among the most vital tasks of the Christian college teacher/mentor/discipler is vision casting. Christian students need to know the possibilities of service at every level, including the leadership levels of all the professions. Some students need to be mentored toward becoming the best, most godly, most influential, and most productive kindergarten teachers possible. Some need to be encouraged to understand the possibility of becoming an equally proficient book or newspaper editor, or filmmaker, or corporate executive, or even secretary of state. We are much better at producing kindergarten teachers than we are at producing servant leaders in other areas of the arts, business, and the professions. We need to do so much better. This is not because good kindergarten teachers are not terribly needed, or because they are less valued than others who might be serving in a more prestigious role, but rather because all Americans, at every level, deserve the opportunity to see competent, caring, committed Christians, and the kind of truth and value judgments Christians are supposed to be offering. Unless our Christian families, churches, and educational institutions commit to this, we will continue to be far less than we should be.

A chief role for faculty mentors is not only to help students see the possibilities of service at every level, but also to raise significantly their understanding of what is expected of them as recipients of an expensive Christian college education and, more than that, as followers of Christ. The idea that American Christians can have the tremendous benefits of living in America, freedom of worship, unprecedented financial prosperity, and a Christ-centered education without a deep sense of responsibility to use all of this in service would have been beyond belief for the past generations. This may seem arcane or esoteric to many these days, but the very heart of the gospel is the idea that we as Christians are not our own, but we have been "bought with a price." The whole idea of the Christian faith is one of redemption. To redeem something connotes paying for it. Christians are always and ever in a debt of love. We owe more than we can ever repay, but it is one of the great paradoxes of our faith that the greatest joy comes from doing all we can all the time to repay this never shrinking debt. Parents, pastors, and college mentors need to reinforce this concept over and over.

Not too long ago, there was a time when dedication to service was much more the norm for Christians. Parents dedicated their children in solemn ceremonies to lives of service to God, and they saw this as their greatest joy. In the 1950s and 1960s there was still a tremendous emphasis on commitment to "full-time Christian service" on the campuses of America's Christian colleges. Sadly, disastrously for the church and our country, much of this philanthropic attitude has disappeared. Now, Christian parents want foremost for their children to be "happy." The emphasis on campus is the good job, building a successful career, and living the good life. Get a job, get a house, get a boat, take a cruise. Because I have spent a lifetime in business, many students from the Christian college near my home come to me for career counseling. When I ask them why they have chosen to pursue a particular career, the most common answer I receive is, "I think it would be fun." Fun! The whole idea of choosing a career to meet a need or fulfill an obligation in a life of sacrificial service in order to repay a debt and serve the country is a very foreign concept. Christians everywhere should be embarrassed and ashamed that secular Americans think more often about Peace Corps service than Christians do about a life of service to which they are very directly and specifically called by God.

It is important to understand that the service I am discussing here is not the professional ministry—the pastorate, a foreign missions assignment, full-time work with a parachurch organization, the Salvation Army, and so on. Rather, it is the service to which every Christian is called as he or she pursues whatever career in which they might be engaged. The Christian physician, lawyer, politician, scientist, publisher, athlete, teacher, plumber, builder, soldier, housewife, or salesperson must see their career not as an end in itself but as an entry point for service to Christ and ministry to his creation. By being there in a particular job setting, Christians have built-in contact with their peers on the job. As we perform our jobs to the very best of our abilities and demonstrate genuine caring for our coworkers, we win a hearing for the things we believe, the ideas and values that inform our Christian faith and which we believe will benefit our colleagues and our country. We must be certain that no opportunity to offer these values goes unfulfilled. We must be committed and ready. We must understand that we are called to this because this is the essence of the Great Commission (see Matt. 28:18–20). We cannot consider ourselves to be obedient Christians and do otherwise. Christian parents, pastors, and especially Christian mentors must impress upon young believers that living accordingly is not a call for anything unusual or heroic, but rather it is our "reasonable service," a very normal expectation. Given how far we have moved from that ideal, this is a lesson not easily taught or caught. This is no reason not to begin. On the contrary, it should be seen as an urgent call to begin. Our country deserves it, and our faith demands it.

As a part of the effort to raise the expectation level for students in Christian colleges, it is most important to paint a realistic picture of what a life of obedient service will look like. Thankfully, and very truthfully, an accurate picture of an obedient Christian life would reflect a life filled not necessarily with fun or happiness but with joy. An obedient Christian life is a wonderful, bright, triumphant life of immense satisfaction. It is not always an easy life, but it is a joyful one. In a fallen world, there are no easy lives. Some jobs or lifestyles may appear glamorous and carefree, but having spent a lifetime in close association with the rich and famous, I have seen that even these live very hard lives. Consider the suicides, murders, drug addiction, constant failed marriages, and other great personal traumas associated with the sports and entertainment communities. For Christians, a life of obedient service is not really about what one gives up, but what one gains. We have done a very poor job of conveying this truth to our own Christian young people and an even worse job of conveying this to our fellow Americans. I am very afraid a Gallup or Barna poll would reveal that very few Americans would even think of, let alone describe the Christian life as joyful, cheerful, triumphant, and ultimately satisfying. We have done such a poor job of letting other Americans see Christ and know who we are as his followers. The prevailing view is that we are down, morose, combative, and judgmental. We have allowed ourselves to be represented in most public arenas mostly by cartoons and caricatures. Far too few Americans have seen a full-blown, fully dimensional obedient Christian up close and personal. This means that we have denied them the right to make an intelligent, informed decision about the benefits of a Christian life for themselves. This is not fair, and it is not the way things should be. Our nation deserves better.

A vital part of making sure that Christian young people understand what is expected of them is to be certain they understand the great, even incalculable, benefits of rising to that expectation. Again, Christian obedience is not about what is lost but about what is gained. The joy to be gained is worth it all. Jim Elliott was a missionary to the Auca Indians of Ecuador and was murdered by some of the Aucas in 1956. In his immortal phrase, "He is no fool who gives what he cannot keep to gain what he cannot lose." All people deserve the opportunity to understand the truth of this.

In raising the level of understanding on what is expected of them, Christian students should also be taught that they will be held accountable. They need to know that upon their graduation, their college, and particularly their mentor, will be following them, tracking them, continuing to offer help and encouragement and seeing if they are being faithful to the mission and to their responsibilities. Are they performing in their business or profession at the optimum level? Most importantly, are they being obedient to Christ and offering Christian truth to those around them? This need not be an onerous undertaking on the part of the college or the mentor. A call or letter once or twice a year to check in should suffice. The college will also gain greatly by having this additional close, personal, and caring contact with alumni. Nine years after graduation from a Christian college, I was given an administrative position with the Miami Dolphins professional football team. I may have been the first graduate of a Christian college in such a position. Not too long after arriving in Miami, my college coach came to see me. He had two basic messages for me: First, the college still cares about you, and second, be faithful and true. He told me not to forget who I was and from where I came. He was both encouraging me and letting me know I was being held accountable for all that had been given to me. Many years later, though as I write this I am nearing retirement age, I still feel accountable. I still want to do my best because I know my coach expects it. Christian colleges need to engender that kind of accountability on the part of many more of their graduates. If that can be done, our graduates and our country will benefit. We will have much less for which to apologize.

American Christians in general and graduates of Christian colleges in particular have a debilitating, irrational, and unwarranted inferiority complex. I think this complex goes back to our love affair with victimhood, a statistically false minority-status feeling. Worst of all, many have a sort of deep-seated belief that our faith is neither rational nor relevant. We are happy to exercise our faith in church and in the Christian subculture, but we are very reluctant to put it to the test in the real world and bring it to bear on the real-world problems of secular Americans. This is totally irrational. The positively changed lives of countless believers throughout the centuries, and often the changes in entire societies as well, should testify to this. There is much empirical evidence that the power of the gospel does work in the lives of men and women. It should be beyond dispute—certainly beyond dispute among Christians. To think otherwise is to operate with a totally unwarranted and sinful inferiority complex.

And yet many Christian college graduates often do lack confidence, and for very real and valid reasons which the colleges need to address. If our graduates are to have a vision of the unlimited possibilities open to them, and if they are to be held accountable for raised expectations, they must be given the tools and the confidence to enable them to succeed in lives of service.

Where I grew up in Texas, there is an old saying that excuses mediocrity. Things are said to be "close enough for government work." Unfortunately, tragically, this same kind of thinking permeates much of Christian higher education (and, not so coincidentally, many other Christian enterprises). Instead of thinking that when we call ourselves by Christ's name it is incumbent upon us, as far as we are humanly able and beyond asking for God's help, to reflect the excellence of the Savior, we say instead, "We are only Christians in a fallen world, so don't expect too much of us." Wrong! With all that we have been given, with all that history teaches us, and, most of all, with the perfect example we have of the One we follow, our fellow Americans should be able to expect the very best we can deliver—every time and all the time. Again, this is our reasonable service. Christian higher education must make a much stronger commitment to excellence if it is to deliver what it should to the church and the

American culture. It is not nearly enough for our graduates to succeed in the Christian subculture. They must be able to succeed in the wider world to have a chance of winning a hearing for the gospel, which is the power of God for salvation. Parents, churches, and particularly the institutions of higher education must do a much better job of equipping students.

George Bernard Shaw rarely got it right as far as Christians are concerned. He was a brilliant agnostic and certainly an enemy of the gospel. But in his classic play *Pygmalion* (the musical *My Fair Lady* is based on the play), Shaw teaches some powerful lessons that should be appropriated by every Christian and understood especially by the faculty and staffs of Christian colleges seeking to equip graduates to serve America. Shaw's basic premise is that language, and how we use it, is the single most determinative factor in how a person will be able to relate to his or her society. In other words, if you can speak well and write well, you have automatic entry into even the top echelons of society. If you can't, you are relegated to a level commensurate with your language deficiencies. If you have fine command of the language, you can communicate up and down throughout society without limitations. Without this command, there is a certain ceiling that inevitably you cannot penetrate. Your language skills stop the elevator at a certain floor, and it cannot go higher. Those on higher levels will never hear Christian truth from you, for you will be unable to speak to them.

My business life was spent in professional sports and television production. Because both are considered by most people to be somewhat glamorous, many want careers in them. What most don't understand is that the ability to speak and write effectively is the most necessary prerequisite for entering and succeeding in these fields. It's all about writing and speaking—about communicating effectively. George Bernard Shaw had it right. Christians must also get it right.

Christians are people of words and of the Word, the Bible. In the Bible, Jesus himself is even called the Word. The incarnation is the Word made flesh. Words and good deeds are the only tools we have, and without the right words, good deeds alone can never do the job we are called to do. We must be masters of language and communication if we are to be faithful in building God's kingdom and if we are to serve our country and culture. The fact that many graduates of Christian colleges are far from such mastery is a disgrace and is something for which we need to apologize and repent. The sad fact is that the Christian subculture generally is a bastion of bad grammar and usage. From Christian television and radio to many pulpits and even to Christian higher education, the English language is misused and abused. The message this sends to other Americans is reflected in the notorious *Washington Post* description of Christians that called us "poorly educated and easily led." While this was a horrible and incompetent overgeneralization and was quickly refuted, resulting in an apology from the *Post*, our misuse of the language leads to these kinds of stereotypes. Our ability to serve Christ and country is significantly hampered by any inability we exhibit to speak and write effectively and well.

Christian colleges have very valid reasons why they are not matching the significant research being done at major universities, using exotic equipment and costly, time-consuming techniques. First, they just don't have access to the kind of funding necessary for first-class research. More importantly, this is not their calling. They have a far more important calling to train those who come to their campuses to be the very best possible disseminators of Christian truth they can be, in whatever field they choose to study. There is absolutely no valid reason—none whatsoever—for not ensuring that every graduate leaves campus with the very best thinking and language skills possible. It is a matter of will, resolve, commitment, and the setting of expectations. It is a matter of drawing a very firm line and setting an irreducible standard of excellence. English and rhetoric are not expensive to teach, relatively speaking. These should be among the very highest priorities of every Christian institution of higher learning. This very definitely also includes our theological seminaries and divinity schools, which graduate far too many pastors with less than exemplary grammar skills.

The call here is not to make every graduate write like a Frederick Buechner or a Max Lucado or to make them able to speak like a Chuck Swindoll or an Os Guinness, although more writers and speakers along those lines would be a great blessing to the church and the world. And certainly upper division courses should be available at our colleges for those who show particular interest and talent in writing and speaking and who need additional training and encouragement to help hone their skills. But the call here is for every graduate to have mastered very basic speaking and writing skills to the extent their communication will not restrict their mobility throughout American society and will not render them impotent as they seek to offer the helpful healing message of the gospel. America deserves Christians with high types of language and communication skills. Christian moms and dads, churches and Sunday schools, and particularly our Christian colleges must supply them. This is not too much to ask or to expect.

Not long ago I was on the campus of a college in the Christian tradition, and I was graciously invited to have lunch with the English faculty (pretty heady stuff for this old physical education major). A very bright young professor opened the conversation with me this way: "Where are you living at?" (My editor tells me I shouldn't worry about this sort of thing, but I do!) I have visited many campuses and have communicated with many faculty members and students—both orally and in writing. I have listened to many introductions before speaking in chapel or at a commencement exercise. The point is that I have come to realize any effort to reform the language skills of graduates must begin with the faculty. A very firm and continuous message must be delivered from the top that correct grammar and usage will be expected from all faculty and across the curriculum. The effort must begin with the English faculty, but it cannot end there. All professors in all the disciplines must practice, expect, and require solid correct usage. No class or research work that doesn't deliver the goods should be accepted.

Until this very real problem is adequately addressed, faculty retreats, seminars, and workshops should have an English usage emphasis. Skilled communicators should be brought in to encourage the faculty in their efforts to improve their communications skills and, more importantly, the skills of their students. College presidents could do a great thing by buying each of their faculty members one of the easily usable and inexpensive guides to good usage.

To Christians professionally involved in Christian higher education, this may seem judgmental and overly pedantic. I do not mean to be that way. And certainly I want to acknowledge again that not all Christian colleges are the same. I have observed that some of the schools— Calvin College, Wheaton College, Taylor University, and Biola University among them—are already doing commendable things in this area and insisting on a high standard of English usage among professors and students.

There may well be other schools that have given this equally serious attention. Much more needs to be done, however, if graduates of our Christian colleges and universities are to have any chance of communicating effectively across the board to our fellow Americans.

In George Bernard Shaw's fine play *Pygmalion* (I show *My Fair Lady,* the filmed musical version of the play, in many leadership classes I teach), Professor Henry Higgins takes Miss Eliza Doolittle, someone literally from the gutter, and tries to teach her to speak, dress, and behave so as to fool all the Royals at the Embassy Ball into thinking she really belongs. Of course, the professor's plan succeeds brilliantly. American Christians desperately need to be able to go to their own "Embassy Balls" to show they really do belong and have much to contribute to the culture.

We need to be there, not for our own pleasure, self-aggrandizement, or to "get ahead." We need to be there to offer the message of Jesus Christ to our fellow Americans who are there. There are the equivalents of "Embassy Balls" in every profession, every academic discipline, and every business career in every geographic area. At least some Christians must be attending. Our ticket to these affairs must be professional competence, our ability to use the language, and impeccable manners with a general sense of style and class.

I am so proud and pleased that our son-in-law and daughter are insisting that their three sons use correct grammar, display proper manners, and dress appropriately. In a recent phone call, I asked the oldest (now eleven) what he was doing. He said he was writing thank-you notes for recently received birthday gifts! These guys are "all boys," enjoying hockey, baseball, basketball, and soccer, as well as hunting and fishing.

Good English and grammar and appropriate dress have not cramped their style.

Parents, churches, and particularly Christian colleges must begin systematically to address this in both curricular and extracurricular ways. Style and "class" must be modeled and mentored. The language problem is so desperate and so foundational, it must be addressed first and with the most rigor. The rest should follow. Our foreign service officers are given extensive training in protocol the better to allow them to communicate effectively to and with the people in their host countries. A similar rationale should motivate and inform a similar effort on the part of our colleges.

Christian colleges and universities, if they are to serve America more effectively, must give urgent thought to what this should mean for the curriculum. It cannot be business as usual. The "this is the way we have always done it" attitude won't work because fundamental changes are needed on the basis of social need as well as the admonition of Jesus to be "salt" in our world. Curriculum change always makes faculty uneasy. Changing the curriculum means altering perspectives and additional class preparation. Old course lecture notes and stale syllabi will no longer suffice. So be it. New, fresh, innovative, relevant teaching is desperately needed. Christian faculty must supply it in the context of the most carefully thought-out, targeted curriculum possible.

Designing a curriculum with America's real needs in mind will mean both new courses and new ways of teaching courses old and new. V. James Mannoia, president of Greenville College, has said that courses in Christian liberal arts colleges must be taught with the idea of offering real solutions to real problems. This is entirely in keeping with the belief that Christianity is relevant to all of life and not something to be compartmentalized in a sort of "Sunday box." Thinking Christians know that the Bible has great wisdom and truth for every social question from a fair tax code to welfare, from homelessness to addiction, from crime and punishment to public transportation issues, and far, far beyond. Christian college students must be taught from this perspective. The facts in a vacuum are not enough. The facts need to be right, but they also need to be applied biblically to real-world problems. This is not easy, but it is essential if we are to serve and help our students and our society in a truly Christian way. When we have failed to show up at the "Embassy Balls," or been unable to offer Christian solutions in less than the best, most compelling way, we have failed America.

One of the paradoxes for which Christians will have to answer is that the things about which we complain the loudest are the things about which we do the least to change. It is always much easier to complain than it is to do the real work of effecting change or of offering alternatives to troubling things. Christian colleges must begin to confront this dilemma in the curriculum.

We complain loud and long about the secular, mainstream press, yet only a small number of Christian colleges even offer journalism majors to prepare graduates to enter the field. I applaud Milligan College, in Johnson City, Tennessee, Point Loma Nazarene University, in San Diego, California, and Regent University, with its new Washington, D.C., journalism program for providing quality journalism majors for their students. I am particularly thankful for the Fieldstand and Company Foundation, which funds an innovative, high quality, real-world journalism experience in our nation's capital for students from Christian colleges and universities. As admirable as these programs are, they are almost totally inadequate in meeting a very huge need for Christian journalists who have the competence, character, class, and commitment to serve on our nation's newspapers and magazines. In the newsrooms of papers large and small throughout the country few offer a Christian perspective on the day's news and how it should be covered. We should not be surprised that the news coverage is often slanted or biased. This is our own fault. We failed to prepare and show up in the field of journalism, and the results are predictable. As our Christian colleges fail to build quality journalism majors on the campuses and fail to emphasize the need to serve in this vital field, the results will continue to disappoint. We will continue to show that we have the heart to criticize without the heart to help. This is not a very viable Christian position.

Perhaps even more than the press, we Christians love to complain about television. As I have traveled to speak in many venues around the country, I've heard many Christians make their case against television. They ask, "Why do you rarely, if ever, see real, authentic Christians portrayed on the major networks' prime-time programs?" This is an easy one to answer: It is because the people who write and produce these shows rarely see a real, authentic Christian. If they desperately wanted to build an entire show around a Christian character, they wouldn't know how to do it, simply because they have no point of reference. Again, we have not shown up in the field of television, and, again, our evangelical schools are doing almost nothing to help the situation. Only Biola University in La Mirada, California, and Regent University, in Virginia Beach, Virginia, have programs that attempt to address this need in any practical and professional way. Much more emphasis needs to be placed on television in the curricula of Christian colleges.

The fields of journalism and television are the two most glaring deficiencies in the curriculum on our

Christian college campuses as they relate to optimum service to our church and country, but there certainly are others. Fine arts, business, and communications emphases are present on most of the campuses, but these areas need significant infusions of quality and a much clearer vision for service to America.

Christian colleges and universities are an incredibly significant educational resource for the church and for all of America. Their potential is very great, if only partly realized. College trustees, administrations, faculty, supporting denominational constituencies, and the alumni themselves must do some urgent and serious reevaluation of programs and priorities if our colleges' fantastic and wonderful possibilities for service to the church and the nation are to be realized. We can't afford the status quo.

In *The Scandal of the Evangelical Mind*, Mark Noll makes what I regard as an irrefutable case that everyone is injured by an evangelical lack of involvement in the intellectual life of America. I would like to make a slightly different point relative to Christian intellectuals. While it is absolutely true that there is a very damaging and acute shortage of Christian thought leaders, it is equally true that we do not fully appreciate or come close to using fully the talents of the intellectuals we do have for optimum service to America. Better deployed Christian intellectuals could make a much more important contribution to American life and thought than is currently the case, and at the same time their higher profile could encourage more bright young Christians to pursue the life of the mind.

While they are far too few in number, we can be very thankful that our Christian scholars and intellectuals are indeed brilliant. The fact that they are relatively few makes it imperative that their skills and insight be used strategically for maximum service to God and country. We cannot afford to have our artists, writers, thinkers, and teachers talking only to one another or writing only for other Christians. The country at large needs and deserves to have their perspectives on a regular, continuing, and public basis, addressing the most pressing and important questions of the day. We need to get evangelical scholars out of the religious subculture and into the mainstream culture. They need to leaven the nation's discourse with their biblically based insights.

Other American intellectuals of the non-Christian variety offer their views much more regularly and systematically to the nation than do our Christian intellectuals. They offer their opinions on broadcast talk shows, in op-ed editorials, and in so-called "think pieces" in major magazines. Many of their writings, often issued by major secular book publishers, capture the attention of and have an important impact on the thinking of America. Our Christian intellectuals need to begin to follow a similar pattern regarding seeking national platforms. With so much that is going on of a religious dimension in our nation and the world, for good and for bad, Christian scholars have unique and valuable knowledge and insights to offer. They need to be more proactive in making their expertise available.

The networks always go to the same two or three cartoon pastors when they want the "Christian" position on the issues of the day. This may be done because they are unaware there are more qualified people to speak on behalf of the American evangelical movement. Or they may do this because consciously they want to highlight people who are sometimes an embarrassment to themselves and, often, the larger Christian cause. But why should the nation be forced to listen to those who will always go out of their way to be in front of a camera when we have highly qualified and articulate intellectuals whose gifts can be of real help to the church and the country? The rest of us need to be much more supportive and helpful in an effort to give brilliant Christians the best possible platforms from which to speak to and serve the nation. Secular foundations and people of means fund the aptly named "think tanks" that provide financial, logistical, and credibility support to allow other intellectuals to speak and publish. Christian foundations, denominations, and parachurch organizations need to support Christian intellectuals in exactly the same way, making sure that the object is to reach not other Christians but the nation at large with the intellectual firepower of the church. The impact could be tremendous. Until we begin to exploit the intellectual talent God has given us in service to the nation, we will continue to fail.

In using the better minds of Christian intellectuals, it is encouraging to note that we can offer the nation intellectual brilliance delivered by articulate and relentlessly equipped theologians, philosophers, scholars, and intellectuals who can more than hold their own before radio microphones and television cameras. Think of only a select number: Harold O. J. Brown, J. Budziszewski, D. A. Carson, Os Guinness, Nathan Hatch, Carl F. H. Henry, Phillip E. Johnson, Richard Land, George M. Marsden, Mark Noll, Marvin Olasky, Alvin Plantinga, David F. Wells, Dallas Willard, and John D. Woodbridge. They, and many others like them, are knowledgeable of the Christian perspectives on the national cultural issues and are comfortable before large audiences, live or electronic. Not to encourage their use in service to the whole nation is very poor stewardship indeed.

Hardly anyone denies that the quality of public education in this country has declined precipitously in the past five decades. There is just too much hard evidence to think otherwise. The statistical comparisons with other industrialized nations are devastating, and in the end our kids just aren't measuring up. It is much easier to measure the decline than it is to analyze the reasons for it, and it is much easier to cast blame for the problem than it is to begin fixing it. With something so vast and diversified as America's schools, complexity is a given. Having said this, there is at least one overreaching reality, which may or may not have a direct cause-and-effect relationship to the current sad state of affairs, that must be recognized: Christians and Christian ideals once dominated the educational system in this country, and now they don't. Christians were once nearly ubiquitous in the educational policy establishment. Now, they are almost totally absent.

Scholars and public policy analysts can delineate the sociological and philosophical changes that resulted in the devolution from conservative, Christian influence in the public schools to a dominant worldview perspective that is almost totally liberal, secular, and humanistic. We all know this occurred and that the schools are now what they are. Would the situation in public education somehow be different and better if Christians had hung in there in leadership strength commensurate with their numbers? We will never really know because, as in so many other areas, many of us abandoned rather than faced the problem. In doing this, we have failed America.

Christians never really left education. What we left, for the most part, was educational *leadership*. While many Christians left public education for private education, there are still many thousands of Christian teachers, administrators, and librarians in this country, all serving in our public schools. In many ways they are heroes, quietly soldiering on, trying to do a good job in a regime operating on a belief system almost totally at odds from theirs. As with so many other areas of American life, the influence of Christians in public education is stunningly small relative to our numbers. Evidently, over recent decades many Christians decided that the battles for leadership in the National Education Association and other teachers' unions, along with important parallel library associations, were not worth the effort or the aggravation. This has been tragic for America, not so much because Christians lost control, but because we have not been there to offer alternative ways of thinking about educational psychology and policy for the children of our nation. When Christians left areas of educational leadership, the vacuum was almost instantly filled by those with completely opposite views. The result was a pell-mell rush toward the public-education mess we now have on our hands. Christians have not been there to slow the changes. And now we are left to complain loudly and with little effect, mostly from the outside.

Even if the first steps are small and slow, thinking, obedient Christians with a missionary calling must begin to return to the organizations which control so much of the educational policy in this country. The education departments in Christian colleges and universities should begin to prepare and inspire those majoring in education to do this. The many organizations of Christian public school educators, which have sprung up in many states as well as nationally, should abandon their isolationist and protectionist agendas and adopt a policy of encouraging their members to begin making a difference in the mainstream establishment organizations. None of this will be easy, but it is possible.

I am inspired by the tenacity and obedience of an evangelical Christian woman who is a member of the Florida Library Association, one of the most liberal of the mainstream educational organizations. She could have done what many Christians have done, become disgusted with the policies of her professional association and simply dropped out. Instead, she made a determined and prayerful decision to hang in, to be of use and the best member she could, and to rise in the ranks until she had the clout to make a difference. Her plan worked beautifully. She eventually obtained the power to name speakers for the association's huge statewide convention. The year before, disgusting shock-jock Howard Stern and a spokesman for the ACLU were the main speakers. In her year, she chose Christian sociologist and popular speaker Tony Campolo, along with yours truly. My topic was the management methods of Jesus. Instead of vulgarities from Howard Stern and superliberal platitudes from the ACLU, hundreds of Florida librarians heard erudite, cogent Christian thinking from Tony Campolo, and the relevance of Jesus to what librarians and educators do from me. The point is, this woman hung in. She was obedient to the command to be salt and light, to make a difference, and to strike a blow for the kingdom. I hope her story will inspire other Christians in education to do the same.

In addition to the wonderful librarian in Florida, many other Christians and Christian organizations are serving both America and the church in wonderful ways in the field of education. I would not want to leave this topic without mentioning some of them and without soliciting reader support for them. Unfortunately, while many are out there, still they are far too few.

In my view, perhaps the single most effective Christian organization in America, the one which makes its resources do the most and go the farthest, is one that operates all over the country in America's public schools. It is called Young Life, a ministry headquartered in Colorado Springs. One Young Life staff person, usually a sharp, "with it," recent college graduate, and one with a deep commitment to the person of Jesus Christ, can transform an entire public high school. I've seen it happen.

I had the privilege of watching a new Young Life staffer operate in a typical suburban high school in the Dallas area. This was a young lady, weighing barely a hundred pounds, and fresh out of Baylor University. She came to work in this high school with no staff colleagues, no coworkers, no office, and no support system—other than a few concerned and committed parents. By simply being on campus, being present at the various games, cheerleading tryouts, band concerts, and even eating in the school cafeteria, this young missionary to high school students built relationships one by one. She showed the students she cared for them and that they could trust her. As the level of trust increased, she began patiently to share the claims of Christ with her new friends. She never rejected the ones who refused these claims, but she continued to be their friend and to be there for them. The ones who accepted Christ and committed themselves to him were given the opportunity to study the Bible in depth and to learn what it had to say about the things that mattered most to them. These things included peer pressure, feelings of loneliness, rejection, depression, problems with parents, drugs, teenage sex, and drinking.

By year two of her stay on campus, many students, including some of the school leaders, were studying the Bible with her—football players, the student body president, even the girl chosen as "most beautiful." Many grew deeper in their Christian faith at Young Life summer camps and ski camps. Now, several years out, many of those kids who were from non-Christian homes, who had never before heard the gospel or been shown its relevance, are now pillars in their churches. Several of them have gone on into Young Life and other Christian ministries themselves. This example is not unique or even unusual at high schools with a Young Life program. It is typical. Even parents who think it is absolutely necessary to home school their children, and churches that think it is necessary to have their own private Christian schools, should work with and support a program like Young Life in their local high schools. That is a way to serve America and not fail her.

Moms in Touch is a prayer ministry for the public schools of America. Mothers of public school students gather in one of their homes each week, never on campus, in order to pray by name for their children, teachers, and principals. They are committed to one thing—prayer. It is prayer focused on their particular children and their schools. They don't do fund-raising, they don't hold events, and they don't support other causes. They pray. They are a wonderfully inspiring group of Christian women who do not fail America.

Two other campus organizations, InterVarsity Christian Fellowship and Campus Crusade for Christ, continue to do wonderful and successful work on the campuses of our nation's public and private universities. They nurture and disciple Christian students and faculty members, and both ministries present the gospel in many effective ways.

Programs such as the Veritas Forum and Christian Leadership are inspiring because they bring Christian intellectuals into the debate arena at the great universities' campuses to go head-to-head with opponents of Christianity in open forums. By sponsoring such powerful Christian apologists as Os Guinness, Phillip E. Johnson, Richard Keyes, John Warwick Montgomery, J. P. Moreland, Clark Pinnock, and Ravi Zacharias on the nation's campuses, the gospel is communicated very effectively, while the open forums serve America in wonderful ways.

I have been quite impressed with the way some Christian denominations have built and staffed facilities either right on university campuses or immediately adjacent to them. In this way, they serve their own denomination's students, but really they are also there to serve all who are interested. Baptist Student Ministries with their Baptist Student Unions are particularly effective and widespread in this regard. The time I have spent working on campus with the students and staffs of the BSUs has shown me some really impressive frontline Christians who serve America.

If you are part of a church in a college or university town and want to serve our country, you will want to know of the First Baptist Church in Tallahassee, Florida. This church should serve as a model for many churches in college and university towns. It commits resources, including full-time staff, to ministering on the campus of Florida State University. Just because FSU is recognized as one of the nation's most notorious "party schools" (maybe because of this), First Baptist did not run away from the campus. Rather, the church sends its own troops in there to seek and to serve. Their work among the great athletic teams at FSU is particularly impressive and inspiring. Many Seminole football and baseball stars have been confronted with the claims of Christ during their time on campus. Because of this church's ministry, many now serve him.

The overall record for Christians' involvement in American education is not a pretty one. Most of us have not served our country very well or as faithfully as the aforementioned groups are trying so hard to do. We need to emulate them. We can turn things around. We can do better. We must do better.

CHAPTER 4

The Politics of Victimhood and the Master's True Business

"Every time the church has gotten into the political game, it has been drawn into betrayal and apostasy. Politics is the church's worst problem. It is her constant temptation, the occasion of her greatest disasters, the trap continually set for her by the Prince of this world."
—Jacques Ellul

MANY FAIR-MINDED AMERICANS WERE RIGHTFULLY resentful when the *Washington Post* described Christians as "poor, badly educated and easily commanded." And yet, we would be hard pressed to refute the claim that we must be very slow learners indeed as it relates to our involvement in politics. After all, the attempts to teach us began with Jesus himself. Every time the Lord's disciples tried to draw him into a political discussion, he knocked them back. He kept insisting he was about a kingdom not of this world. The disciples finally learned the lesson. None of them ever led anything approaching a political movement. Evidently, many contemporary American Christians, and especially many of their church leaders, still have not learned the lesson. Because of this, we often fail America and fail her very badly.

When the church fails our country by ill-advised, ill-conceived, antiscriptural involvement in politics, the failures are not insignificant and easily reversed. They are huge, long lasting, and extremely difficult to overcome. Our involvement in politics, particularly over the past twenty years, has created negative images and stereotypes in the minds of millions of people all across the country. It will take decades to erase these images. Because of this ill-advised political involvement, many in our country see Christians as being on a mission far different from the one Jesus actually was on and directed his followers toward. This obscures the real message of the gospel and makes it much more difficult to win a hearing for it. Again, the country loses.

As some of our most visible Christian pastors and leaders pursue a political agenda, a number of things happen, and all of them are bad. The first thing that happens is that the discourse between these people and the nation the church is trying to reach and serve focuses on everything but the real message Jesus sent us to offer. Syndicated newspaper columns, radio and television talk shows, and letters to the editors of important newspapers all focus on the politics of conservative Christians rather than the message of the Christian gospel. We get the kind of headlines like the one over Al Hunt's *Wall Street Journal* column which said, "The Religious Right Is

About Politics Not Faith." In the column itself, Hunt says this: "Some of the notorious voting guides put out by the Christian Coalition and others—which supposedly gauge a candidate's commitment to people of faith—are even more egregious. In the last election in California, for example, candidates were deemed less committed to faith if they voted against term limits or a Constitutional amendment making it harder to raise taxes nor medical savings accounts. The guides never gave scriptural citations. In Texas, the religious right was more extreme. Among the 'Christian' issues candidates were judged on were a state sales tax on motor vehicles and training teachers to teach phonics in schools."

The *WSJ* writer ended this particular column this way: "Demagoguing and religion aren't a new combination in Texas. More than half a century ago, Texas Governor Pappy O'Daniel crusaded for English-only in the schools, arguing with unfailing logic that if English 'was good enough for Jesus Christ, it's good enough for Texas school children.' Pappy O'Daniel probably knew he was engaging in sophistry; Pat Robertson may not."[3]

This is not the kind of dialogue or exposure the church of Christ needs. We should want the kind of dialogue that gives us the opportunity to graciously bring biblical truth to bear on current topics, presenting them as alternatives to consider, alternatives we firmly believe. In his second letter to the Corinthians, the apostle Paul says that Christ has committed his message of reconciliation to us. "All this is from God, who reconciled us to himself through Christ and gave us the ministry of reconciliation: that God was reconciling the world to himself in Christ, not counting men's sins against them. And he has committed to us the message of reconciliation. We are therefore Christ's ambassadors, as though God were making his appeal through us"(2 Cor. 5:18–20).

Reconciliation, not phonics, is the ultimate message about which Christians need to be concerned. Anything hindering or distorting the gospel message should be avoided like the very plague. When politics does distort the message of Christ, it is in fact a plague.

Nowhere does Scripture instruct God's people to influence governmental policy or to control political power. Instead, Christians are to keep very firmly in mind that the One we love and serve came to bring about a kingdom not of this world but of another. Like political ambassadors, we have very specific orders. Our mission is to be salt and light to the world in which we live. We are to make disciples for the Lord Jesus, and to show him high and lifted up. Being faithful in this mission probably has nothing to do with who controls the White House, the congress, or state and local governments. When we forget this, unseemly things occur, and none of them are good for the church or country.

At one point, we had the puzzling situation where two leading Christian families lobbied congress and the state department on whether or not China should receive most-favored nation status. They took opposite sides! We need always to keep in mind that the Great Commission did not come with a foreign policy portfolio. Our responsibility to Chinese Christians, which both sides on the MFN debate purported to want to protect, is to pray for them, support them financially, as much as possible, and give them all the spiritual help we possibly can. It is not to become lobbying agents for their government, arrogantly claiming we know what is best in a highly complex set of circumstances. It is certainly not to pit American Christians against each other!

When he stays focused on the family, Dr. James Dobson of Focus on the Family is one of the church's and nation's greatest resources. His biblically based ministry to parents and children has served the church and the nation very well. But when this leader wades into the political wars, he becomes a loose cannon. In February of 1998, Dobson addressed the Council for National Policy. The speech was widely covered in the national media, both favorably and unfavorably (division rather than unity is always one of the results of Christians engaging in politics). Sounding amazingly like a biblical prophet seeking to anoint a king, Dobson said the following. "In 1995, *I* was looking for a politician, a Republican leader, who had a chance to win the White House, who understood what *I* had been saying, who understood that moral foundation to the universe, who was willing to articulate it and willing to fight for it, and *I* decided that Phil Gramm just might be that man" (emphasis mine). Here is the specter of the Christian child psychologist as king maker. In the light of Scripture, in the light of human history, why don't more Christians see both the irony and the futility of this?

After castigating Phil Gramm, Newt Gingrich, Christine Todd Whitman, Bob Dole, Jesse Helms, Bill Clinton, John Ashcroft and the entire Republican Party, Dobson closed his speech with this: "If we simply had a moral leader, or a party of moral leadership, who had the courage like Ronald Reagan did with the Soviets, despite everything the press threw at him for calling it the 'Evil Empire,' if we had people in government who stood up for these things we believe and didn't dance around and try to avoid criticism by the press but went right to the heart of it saying, 'This is right, and I stand on it even if no one believes it,' we could win this thing and we could do it very quickly in my view. What we need are people of courage." When Christian leaders get so deeply involved in this kind of party politics, they really do fail America.

The call for Christians to serve America is not about winning and losing. It is about being obedient to the gospel mission. It is not about taking elected leaders to task. It is about offering people hope and a new way of life. It is not even about morals. Morality is not the end product but rather a by-product of any success we might have in sharing the gospel and winning individuals to Christ. When we aim to change the nation's morals, we never aim high enough. And, of course, we almost never change the morals. Among the most damaging aspects about all strictly political messages delivered by Christian leaders, such as the one just mentioned, is they imply that politics and politicians are the answer to the basic needs of the nation. It suggests that if we only had the right "moral" person in the White House, or a "party of moral leadership" and "people of courage" in power, we could "win this thing." Win what thing? Certainly not a victory for Christ and his cause. This is preposterous, and patently and empirically wrong even if we are only talking about changing mere morals. And changing morals is not our job.[4]

Does it not compute with the Christian political activists that even when we had a Republican administration for twelve years, including eight years with Ronald Reagan, that divorce rates still climbed, alcoholism and drug trafficking increased, pornography became more openly peddled, and other evils generally prospered? Politicians, even moral ones, and political parties can't get it done. Period. To spend time, money, and more importantly, precious good will, in a divisive effort that will not work fails America. It makes the task for obedient Christians doubly difficult.

Do we care whom our president and other elected officials are? Of course we do. Should this change the basic modus operandi of the Christian mission? It should not. If an administration more sympathetic to Christian values is in power, we should be very thankful. But we should be just as diligent about our Master's business. We can never expect a political agenda to heal the land. Only the gospel can do that. We need to be faithful to it, and we need to be a preservative salt in our society. We need to be ambassadors for our King. We need to be making disciples for him. When an administration is in power that we perceive to be unsympathetic to Christian values, what should we do? Stay the course. Our mission does not change. We do not suddenly get new marching orders that call for us to organize politically and put our time and God's money toward an attempt to unseat the new unsympathetic regime. No. All the basics remain the same. The gospel message remains the same. Our task remains the same.

The truth is that the occupant of the White House is relatively unimportant in the eternal scheme of things. What remains desperately important is for Christians to do what we are called to do, to bring the healing and reconciling message of the gospel to as many as will receive it. As Jesus was not oblivious to the evil around him, we are not to be oblivious to the evil around us or to the pain and suffering it causes. Our mistake is in thinking that political power and position are the answers to the world's evil. We should know that in reality Christ is the only answer. There are simple criteria by which we should judge any activity in which we are engaged: Does what I do draw people to Christ, or does it repel them? Does what I do tell people who Jesus is and why he came into human history? Does what I do give people more reason to listen to and accept the gospel, or, as is so often the case with Christian leaders who turn political and alienate many, more reason to ignore and reject it? Honest answers to these questions reveal nearly all political activities by

Christians, especially power plays, arm twisting, king making, and such, fail the test.

The brand of politics practiced by many Christian leaders today is particularly onerous because it damages both the country and the church. It is the politics of victimhood. It seeks to portray Christians as a poor, persecuted minority, impotent in the face of all the evil around us. It whines about our freedoms being "under fire." The reality is that the freedom of Christians is not so much under fire as it is vastly under used. We have more freedom to actually be the church of Jesus Christ than we ever use. The politics of victimhood constantly goes on about betrayal, constantly seeking someone to blame (while failing to acknowledge our own failures as the real culprit). Os Guinness has well expressed a similar complaint:

> Prominent parts of the Western church today, in pursuit of public influence, have abandoned Christ's response to injury and shamelessly promoted a contemporary secular strategy—redress through blaming or playing the victims. Suddenly such Christians have gone from portraying themselves as 'the sleeping giant' of public life to 'the poor little whipping boy' of hostile secular forces arrayed against them.
>
> Shame on such a deliberately chosen strategy! The merciless persecution of Christians in many parts of the non-Western world, simply for professing Christ, is a crime. And there is unquestionably a good deal of anti-Christian bias and prejudice in parts of Western society today; examples are easy to find. But a strategy of victim playing should be unthinkable for followers of Christ. Put simply, it is factually misleading, morally hypocritical, politically ineffective, and psychologically dangerous. Worst of all, it is unfaithful, a deliberate and outright denial of Jesus' teaching and call to suffering and rejection.
>
> Have these Christian leaders no shame? Let them scour the New Testament from beginning to end. They will not find one single line to justify the politics of anxiety and resentment that has characterized parts of their stand in public life recently.[5]

The politics of victimhood and blame are counterproductive in the extreme. With all the blessings of living in this great land at this exciting time in history, do Christians really want to be seen as whimpering, put-upon, downtrodden victims? Is this any way to attract people to the Christian worldview and to our Lord? Will our message of hope, joy, and love be believed? Can we really contribute much of anything to our society while whining and blaming?

Does blaming others for our lack of involvement and our lack of obedience really help or change anything for the better? Do those we blame so vociferously for the problems of our society come running to us for the answers that we haven't ever bothered to offer in the past? Is there anywhere in Scripture that commands Christians to cast blame? There are many very specific scriptural imperatives for Christians, but casting blame and playing victims are not among them.

Politics generally and the politics of victimhood and blame in particular hurt Christians even more than they hurt the nation at large. Ultimately they rob us of the joy of being fully, productively, and positively engaged in the only biblically based effort proven to heal our land. The political "solution" to our nation's problems points us in an absolutely false direction, and victimhood provides us with an all too attractive excuse to be part of the problem rather than the real true solution. Everyone loses.

What might have happened if all that was spent by Christians on a political agenda in the past twenty years—all the time, energy, money, thought, emotions, creativity, media time and expenses, and goodwill—had been spent instead in obedience to clear biblical commands to be salt, to proclaim the good news, and to make disciples? Instead of blaming, what if we had been out there blessing? Instead of playing victim, what if we had been serving and ministering to the real victims in our society? Instead of holding press conferences, what if we had been holding prayer vigils? Instead of haranguing elected officials, what if we had been graciously offering our leaders relevant, cogent, intellectually defensible biblical truth on the issues in the forefront of public discussion? What if we tried to be sources of help instead of sources of irritation? What if we tried helping pave the way for elected leaders on unpopular but correct decisions by doing our job in the public square? What if we had tried to show elected officials on both sides of the aisle and of every political persuasion, from Barney Frank to Jesse Helms, that we actually cared about them as people, as men and women for whom Christ died? What if we could demonstrate we were more interested in their spiritual well-being than in their vote? Knowing how difficult their lives are, what if we had a ministry directed to the families of elected officials?

If we had done these things, would America be the "Christian nation" so many of our Christian political activists seek? Probably not. Scripture tells us that things will continue to get worse until Jesus comes again. But the growth rate of evil could have been slowed, individual hearts and lives would have been transformed by Christ, and there could have been new respect for the gospel throughout the land. The church would have been re-energized, and obedient Christians would have been filled with the joy that comes only from knowing they are truly co-laborers with Christ in the effort to build his kingdom, a kingdom that is emphatically not of this world. And we wouldn't have to be apologizing for failing our country.

Should individual Christians ever be involved in politics? Absolutely and emphatically yes. Christianity is more than just a religion of personal salvation. It involves a fully orbed world-and-life view, and this means we are to be active in the culture war, to do what we can to be good citizens. Scripture commands every Christian to be a good citizen. We should certainly vote for and support good people. And, as a political strategy, it is certainly the right of American citizens, Christians very much included, to petition for and against causes important to us. But do not confuse any of this with our kingdom duties as Christians. Never let what we do politically, as good citizens, supplant or supercede what we are commanded to do by our King. Never begin to think that politics can do the job in the hearts and lives of people that only the gospel can do. To think that we can change the course of history through Christian political activity is sheer folly. To think we can change the hearts of men and women by anything other than Christ is blasphemy. And changing hearts is what true kingdom making is all about.

Jack Kemp, my friend from pro football days, once told me, "Bob, America won't be saved from Air Force One. It can only be done one heart at a time. I just want to be a roaring lamb." Jack gets it. He models the way a Christian should be involved in politics. If called to careers in politics, Christians should serve with excellence, doing and creating as much good as possible, recognizing, as Jack does, the limitations of what statecraft can do as well as the unlimited potential of what the gospel can do. Politics is a very worthy, right, and proper calling for Christians. We need more of our best and brightest minds in the political arena—in all the political parties. The great William Wilberforce, the Christian member of the British Parliament in an earlier century, is another outstanding example of a Christian serving admirably in a demanding political career. A man of great good humor and goodwill, Wilberforce was admired by even his political enemies. He pushed his political beliefs through persuasion, logic, and an appeal to what is right and good—never through threats or power plays. After decades of effort, Wilberforce was successful in seeing the evil of the slave trade outlawed in Great Britain. We need more modern Wilberforces at every level of American politics.

Jack Kemp is not the only Christian leader beginning to understand that neither the church nor the nation is served when Christians abandon our divine mandates for a political one. For one thing, the political mandate removes our "set apartness." Christians have a special role to play in a society, and when they abandon it, everyone loses. The syndicated newspaper columnist Cal Thomas, who is a friend, is one of the most politically astute and involved men in this country. He was once even the vice president of Jerry Falwlell's Moral Majority. In his new book, *Blinded by Might: Can the Religious Right Save America?* written with Ed Dobson, also a former Moral Majority staff member, he now argues against a political agenda for the church.[6] On *Fox News Sunday,* Thomas succinctly delineated the difference. "Politics is about compulsion. The gospel is about conversion." There is a huge difference. Dobson, in an interview in the *Lansing State Journal,* said this about the danger of politics: "You begin to think that the only way to transform culture is by passing another law." He said churches should stay out of politics and stick with what the real gospel prescribes—helping individuals and serving their communities. Dobson, a native of Northern Ireland, also said that we have politicized the gospel with our agendas. To some, this means that to be a real Christian, you must be a Republican. That is heresy, according to Dobson, and only a short distance from the extremism of Irish counterparts. Dobson's advice to Christians: By all means register to vote and become a part of the political process. But when Pat Robertson and other preachers with political aims appear on television to ask for money, go volunteer to ladle broth in a soup kitchen instead.

No one was more deeply involved in high-level politics than Chuck Colson during the Nixon administration. There are few today who are as insightful about the process as he is. These days, however, as a committed Christian, Colson sees politics through the lens of Scripture. He has said on many occasions that religious leaders are those most easily seduced by political power. This is because they justify their actions by assuming they are advancing God's purposes. The results are often moral arrogance, pride, self-importance, hypocrisy, and excess. Often when Christians organize politically, the rules that are supposed to govern their behavior individually seem not to apply collectively. And so we find that much of the fuel driving modern day Christian activism is anger, bitterness, and resentment. As Os Guinness would say, "shame on us."

Pulitzer Prize-winning author Anna Quindlen, who writes for the *New York Times*, helps us to understand the whole question of abortion and the problem of Christian political activism. She was discussing all the abortion activities, pro and con, and said of Christians, "They are wasting their time and ours. The venue is not the streets or even the womb. It is the mind." Quindlen is only partly correct. Most of the rhetoric, demonstrations, and political posturing certainly have been a great waste of time. But the venue is not the mind. It is the heart, and only the message of Jesus Christ changes hearts. The Christian's only real, solid, positive, and productive response to any evils of the world, including abortion, is the cross of Christ and the Christ of the cross.

Some of the most highly influential policy shapers in Washington, D.C., are almost completely unknown to the public. They don't hold high office. They don't have radio shows, or appear on television talk shows, or hold press conferences. Only very rarely do they even speak in public. If you are visiting our nation's capitol, you might see one of them in the Executive Office Building, at the Supreme Court, at the Pentagon, in the Capitol itself, or in one of the other governmental buildings in the District. You might mistake one for a senator, a member of Congress, or a cabinet secretary. They would be impeccably dressed and have an air of belonging.

To the extent they operate from anywhere, it is from a large home with spacious grounds very discreetly located at the end of a cul-de-sac just across the Potomac from the District. If you were to visit the main house or the guest house, you might recognize national or international political figures coming and going, or engaging in quiet conversations on park benches or strolling along one of the paths.

The early leaders of this group moved to Washington more than thirty years ago, mostly from the Pacific Northwest. The major influence in their lives was Mark Hatfield, then a newly elected senator from Oregon. In many ways, their spiritual leader was the late Richard C. Halverson, then pastor of The Fourth Presbyterian Church in Bethseda, Maryland, and later to be elected Chaplain of the United States Senate. I won't even mention the names of those still active in this important group of policy shapers. Anonymity and confidentiality are hallmarks of all they do. They don't even like for people to know the name of their organization. You won't get any fund-raising appeals from them.

Yet they are responsible for one very big, very public event, the Presidential Prayer Breakfast. They are invisible at the event. Of the hundreds who attend, almost no one knows how it is put together or how it is run. It is a massive undertaking, and none of the people who make it happen take any bows. To the ones who operate from the discreet property across the Potomac, the Prayer Breakfast is, in many ways, the least important of the things they do. Far more important to them are the very private times of prayer and Bible study they have in the office of an elected official, or with a military officer at the Pentagon, or with people who work at the Supreme Court. These were the men who showed up at the prison where Chuck Colson was incarcerated to present the gospel to him. They were the ones who rallied around a senator from the Midwest when alcoholism threatened to destroy him and his family. There are no photo-ops with these behind-the-scenes Christian operatives, no press leaks, no tell-all memoirs. They are not lobbying for legislation, or looking for jobs, or trying to influence any political or party agendas. They are not about king making. They already have a King. It is the Lord Jesus. They are in Washington to serve him and those important to him, which is everyone from the President of the United States to the House pages. Their influence for both time and eternity is enormous.

May God bless them and others like them, and may he show us that the silent servant or the invisible servant is perhaps the very best political model for Christians to imitate.

CHAPTER 5

Salting Our World Through the Media and the Arts

AMERICA IS MEDIA MOLDED, ENTERTAINMENT ENTHRALLED, and far more affected by the arts than most Christians realize. To the extent that Christians have failed to take our appropriate place and exercise our appropriate influence in the arts, we have failed America. Since culture is America's most important export, we have also failed the world.

Evangelical Christians are more severely underrepresented in media, entertainment, and the arts than in almost any other aspects of American life. The fault is ours. No one has kept us out. No one has organized against us, or put up any non-scalable barriers for us to climb. For the most part, we have chosen either to abandon these areas or to ghettoize them. In some fields, such as the movies, Christians are a barely discernible minority. In others, such as music, Christians have created an entire separate industry for themselves and themselves alone. It is separate, but hardly equal. In fact, it is much easier for Christians to "cross over" into mainstream contemporary music than it is for mainstream musicians to enter the Christian music ghetto. Neither the abandonment nor ghettoizing of the arts serves America—or the church.

Historically, Christians dominated the arts. Much of the world's greatest and most enduring music and art were created by Christians to honor God. When Johannes Guttenberg invented movable type in the 1400s, the cutting-edge media technology of its day, it was powerfully co-opted by Christians and the world was blessed. It was blessed not only by much greater access to the Bible, but also by the printing of Christian books, which forms much of the cannon of Western literature. Music, painting, sculpture, architecture, writing, dance, and the dramatic arts were honored by the church and supported by the church and by Christians of wealth because they were seen as ways to honor God and to express love for him and his creative gifts.

What happened? Scholarly treatises can delineate how the Reformation, Puritanism, the Enlightenment, the Protestant work ethic, and many other movements contributed to the situation in which we now find ourselves. For our purposes, it is enough to suggest that when the means, methods, and attitudes that shaped our present media, entertainment, and arts world emerged, Christians ran for cover. In sharp contrast to the way Christians saw movable type as an almost inherently good and wonderful tool to use in telling our stories (in telling the Story), we somehow saw all the new electronic media and mass-produced journalism as inherently evil. When we ran, we left a huge vacuum, a vacuum that was immediately filled by people who had no interest in the Story. The price we are paying and the country is paying for this is incalculable.

Our mandate in this area of the arts comes from the Lord Jesus himself in his most famous, comprehensive, and far-reaching discourse, the Sermon on the Mount (see Matt. 5–7). The admonition that applies is the one to be "salt." The consequences of failing to be "salt" are spelled out so graphically that to be disobedient should be unthinkable for Christians who are interested in this field. The church as a whole and each of its individual members are called to be "salt," a preservative element in our world and in the creative community. When we fail, Jesus says we are worthless and fit for nothing but to be thrown out and trampled underfoot. What an indictment for those of us who are disobedient! And yet few Christians have any sort of regular, ongoing, systematic plan to be obedient in this area. The same is true of most local churches. Most churches will at least have some sort of plan on paper for proclaiming the gospel and for making disciples, the other two-thirds of the most important scriptural imperatives, but almost none will have any sort of impetus for obedience in this vital field of the arts. As a result, the nation and the church lose big time.

Being the salt Jesus admonishes us to be is a separate and distinct act of obedience. It is neither proclamation nor discipling per se. But it does help prepare the way for the effectiveness of both, and it helps to lay a foundation for both. Being salt is introducing the ideas of goodness and righteousness where they are lacking. And they are certainly lacking in much of American society—this is especially true in the media and entertainment worlds—because Christians have done a poor job of salting our world. Media, entertainment, and the arts should be the most useful and consistently used vehicles for Christians to use in reaching our society, but we have made only the barest, most minimal use of them. As a result, we have seen a breathtakingly fast erosion of many of the basic values on which the country was founded and which were once taken for granted by a vast majority of Americans. In so many ways, the press, the film industry, television, and the arts (particularly music) define and shape the core values of our society. Unfortunately, the family, church, and school no longer play as large a role as they once did in defining these values. With Christians basically absent from so much of mainstream communications, it should be no surprise that biblical values are also basically absent. This is no one's fault but our own.

To better understand the role of media relative to the biblical command to be salt, we can be very thankful there exist some positive examples, far too few though they may be. The prime-time television dramas *Touched by an Angel* and *Promised Land,* though never proclaiming the gospel message in detail, are very "salty" expressions indeed. These programs are both produced by a Christian writer named Martha Williamson. They introduce into prime-time television the whole idea of a personal, caring God who is involved in human affairs. They extol goodness and denounce evil and promote personal kindness and sympathy while telling compelling stories. Martha Williamson shows us we should not make excuses for being disobedient in our own spheres of influence. She shows it can work, even in that toughest of all milieus— prime-time television.

Surprisingly, sometimes stunningly, *Walker, Texas Ranger,* another prime-time television show, is even bolder in the way its story lines honor God and virtue. Chuck Norris, the producer and star, is another very positive example. When Christians are obedient, the "salt" helps prepare the way, makes the gospel itself more accessible, and, as it is embraced, makes discipleship possible. Some sow, others water, still others reap.

Because Christians have been so negligent in sowing "salt" into our society, especially via the media, entertainment, and the arts, evangelism has become very difficult. There are so few Martha Williamsons and Chuck Norrises out there laying at least some sort of basic foundation for a personal God, that anyone trying to do evangelism has to start from so far back that it is extremely hard. This is why only Billy Graham, and to a lesser extent Luis Palau, even attempt the kind of mass evangelism that was so much a part of the American landscape only thirty or forty years ago. For people without a basic Judeo-Christian understanding and a commitment to a core of values, which includes some understanding of absolute truth and a personal responsibility to it, most evangelistic messages are incomprehensible and therefore ineffective. Without the "salt," it doesn't work—at least not the way God intends. Without obedient Christians performing our very specific role of being the "salt" in the fields where God calls us, the country is much poorer.

For Christians to be obedient, it is not necessary for our message to dominate. We don't need to seek control of all the means of communication, the way dictators do when they come to power. We don't even need to directly attack messages that are out there in blatant opposition to ours. We do, however, very much need to give our fellow Americans a choice of messages. Presently, the Christian message is so scarce, so spasmodic, and often so poorly delivered that we really are not being fair. We are not giving our fellow Americans a real opportunity to choose. We want them to appreciate the Christian perspective, but we don't tell them how or why. It is not nearly enough to produce a *Chariots of Fire* or a *Christy* every twenty-five years, or to produce two or three hours of prime-time television a week. We need to be much more regular, intentional, systematic, and strategic in our thinking and in our obedience if we are to serve the nation the way we should.

When the Iron Curtain came down and Eastern Europe suddenly became open to the gospel, the church in America responded in an extraordinary and unprecedented way. Almost all the major Protestant denominations, as well as the leading parachurch organizations, such as Campus Crusade for Christ, Navigators, World Vision, and so on, came together to respond to the tremendous opportunity. These ministries put aside their parochial interests and really joined together in a well-thought-out, highly coordinated effort which came to be called Co-Mission. While this modern-day effort is still very much in progress, it will certainly be regarded as one of the most successful undertakings of Christians throughout all church history.

Something similar to the Co-Mission effort is needed relative to media, entertainment, and the arts in America. Even given the decades of neglect and abandonment, the opportunities for Christians to begin to fulfill our roles in these vital fields has never been greater. It won't be easy, but nothing really worthwhile ever is. The Scripture that I believe describes our current situation is the apostle Paul's comment in 1 Corinthians 16:9, "Because a great door for effective work has opened to me, and there are many who oppose me." Great adversaries, but great opportunities.

Calvin College's Quentin J. Schultze has said that there have never been more opportunities for independent producers, including Christians, to bring programming to television than now. Unfortunately, there has been almost no preparation by Christians to meet these opportunities.[7] Similar opportunities, along with similar obstacles, exist in movies, journalism, and the visual and verbal arts.

The rising popular interest in what the American public sees as a "spiritual" dimension to life is generally being met with New Age or Eastern mysticism journalism and with very popular books in the same vein. Christians, for the most part, have not responded to the opportunity to present biblical truth as a positive answer to the spiritual questions many Americans are asking. Christian writers addressing the situation have generally done it within the Christian publishing ghetto, writing only to the like-minded and almost always from a negative rather than a positive approach, obviously without much impact in the country at large. We need to respond better and more pointedly to these kinds of opportunities to evangelize our world and transform it to reflect the wisdom and creativity of God.

The current situation in the motion picture industry also presents unusual opportunities for Christian film producers. At a time when the number of screens is expanding, the big studios are significantly cutting back on the number of films they are producing. They are now more interested than ever in acquiring distribution rights to independently produced, story-driven films with modest budgets, the very kind of films Christians can and should be producing. We need a Co-Mission type of effort sponsored by the church in America to take advantage of these opportunities and to overcome the obstacles.

Without in any way demeaning some of the very noble efforts by Christians currently contributing to this field, we certainly need a much more concerted effort with sponsorship and involvement from more of the very top leadership of the church. America deserves no less. Obedience requires nothing less. I certainly want to applaud and express thanksgiving for such efforts as are currently being undertaken in journalism by Dean Nelson at Pointe Loma Nazarene University in San Diego. And kudos also goes to Terry Mattingly, the national religion columnist for Scripps Howard, who has also been giving leadership to the summer journalism program of the Council for Christian Colleges and Universities, a program funded by the Fieldstand and Company Foundation. Regent University's new Washington Journalism program shows great promise. The Los Angles Film Studies Institute, another program of the Council for Christian Colleges and Universities, does a terrific job of providing training and field entrée for Christians interested in serving in the motion picture industry. Rick Bee and the Studio Task Force at Biola University, in La Mirada, California, with both their campus programs and their media conferences held around the country, make outstanding contributions particularly in television. The venerable Inter Mission ministry of Hollywood Presbyterian Church has a long and laudable track record of assisting Christians in the movie business or who aspire to a career there. Asbury College, in Wilmore, Kentucky, provides good programs to train students entering the television field.

Among the more interesting and inspirational of these kinds of efforts is Phil Glasgow's Christian comedy college and dinner theatre in Pigeon Forge, Tennessee. Glasgow, a successful entrepreneur, has invested millions of dollars in the very "salty" idea that he can help train a generation of young comics to go out into the comedy clubs and theatres and entertain America with really funny, really wholesome humor. His dinner theatre features excellent food and wonderfully clean comedy presented in a very professional way. Pigeon Forge, like Branson, Missouri, is becoming a destination resort area for those who want to combine a visit to a beautiful area of the country with quality entertainment experiences. These kinds of venues should be able to reach a good cross section of Americans.

Also impressive and worth mentioning is Word Out. Word Out is an effort to produce sixty-second television commercials of the very highest quality that have a Christian message. They say their ministry is "taking the message of Christ to America sixty seconds at a time." Their emphasis is on excellent production to match the prime-time commercials sponsored by any Fortune 500 company. They do very time buying on some of the major networks' most watched programming in order to reach the most Americans with the best message at the most reasonable cost. The people involved have the experience and credentials to make this happen.

As praiseworthy as these and many other quality programs run by Christians are, they are minuscule relative to both the need and the opportunity. We need a Co-Mission effort and commitment. In the best of all worlds, important Christian leaders such as Billy Graham, Bill Hybels, Joe Stowell, Jim Cymbala, Chuck Colson, Bill Bright, Jimmy Draper, Charles Swindoll, Harold Myra, and other top Christian leaders, including denominational heads, could convene a national conference to address the situation. The goal should be to create task forces to explore moving Christians into journalism, radio and television, motion pictures, publishing, music, dance, and the visual arts. They should have action mandates, not just talking ones. It should be made very clear, if it is not already clear, that time should not be wasted on telling one another how bad the current media and artistic climate are. All the energy and all the focus should be on how some of the fabulous creative and material resources of the American Christian church can be used in obedience to our Lord's admonition to be the "salt of the earth."

In 1993, I wrote a book called *Roaring Lambs*, which attempted to address some of these same issues.[8] At that time I felt the greatest need was for writers, writers across the entire spectrum from journalists to novelists to non-fiction writers for radio, television, and the movies. Of course there is still a great need for quality Christian writers, and we can never have too many. But in the last several years I have crisscrossed the country many times speaking and listening to a wide variety of people on the subject, including literally thousands of people who have contacted me personally and individually, and I now feel there is a higher priority, a greater need. It is for Christian business acumen and expertise to be brought to bear on media and the arts.[9]

The Christian creative community, while certainly not large enough or focused enough on meeting scriptural imperatives, is still drastically underserved and undersupported from a business standpoint. We have the terribly unfortunate situation where many of our most creative brothers and sisters in Christ spend up to 90 percent of their time on the business side, raising funds and supporting themselves at a low level, not because they want to, but because they have no other choice. There are no business resources available for them. I am saddened by hearing from many very talented Christians, trying to use their giftedness in obedience, who have no idea how to get their work published, produced, or distributed. I am embarrassed to know writers who are much more talented than I, who can't even get an editor to read their work. There are only a handful of competent Christian literary agents, and their rosters are so full they cannot take on new clients regardless of how talented these writers might be. For creative Christians who aspire to serve in television or the movies, the situation is even much worse.

Ken Wales produced *Christy*, and with the significant backing of Jeff Sagansky, then at CBS, Ken brought it into the homes of millions of Americans. *Christy* paved the way for television series such as *Touched by an Angel*,

Promised Land, and *Seventh Heaven.* Ken worked for seventeen years and made many personal sacrifices before he was able to make the deal for CBS to air *Christy.* He did this as an act of obedience. He felt God had entrusted him with this wonderful project and that he had no choice but to see it reach the public.

Ken is a very sharp and creative guy, but essentially he is a creator, a writer, and a producer, not a businessman. Because for so long there was no one there to help on the business side, he had to do it himself at a great personal sacrifice representing seventeen years of struggle. We are thankful for *Christy* and the impact it continues to make on television, in video, and on PAX in the homes of American families, as well as on the thinking of those who control prime-time television. But because no one helped or supported Ken Wales on the business side, the content of the series was significantly watered down from a Christian perspective. Without strong business and financial backing, Ken simply had to make the content compromises he would not otherwise have made. Sadly, he also had to give away much of the financial reward that should have gone back to him, at least in partial repayment for the seventeen years of sacrifices he made to get the series on the air. The next time you see the show in reruns or on video, watch the credits, and you will begin to understand.

The Heartland Film Festival is held every year in Indianapolis. It is, even by Hollywood standards, a glittering affair with many notables from the movie and television industry showing up to view the family-oriented movies and attend several black-tie events. Many wonderful films are presented. While this is not a Christian film festival, almost all the films entered tend to be the kind of pictures Christians long to see and that all Americans need to see. Many of the films are beautifully done. It is sad to say, however, that almost none will ever be viewed by average American moviegoers. The films have been produced, often very well produced and at great sacrifice, but no one has figured out how to ensure film distribution, the essential business side of getting these movies before the public. Most of them remain in their cans, virtually unseen.

The same is just as true of television. Production of a television program is very difficult. When I ran my company ProServ Television, we used to say that only one of every hundred or so good ideas ever made it into production. And production was by far the easiest part of the process. Distribution and the attendant advertising or underwriting are far more important and far more difficult. I am always grieved when Christians come to me with strong ideas for television programs, sometimes having already spent thousands of dollars on production or preproduction, without having the slightest idea how to get the programs on the air. Few Christians are experienced, equipped, and motivated enough to help in this area.

In my view, Christians in business have drastically underserved the church's creative community. When it comes to their involvement in a productive relationship to media and the arts, they are nowhere. In many ways this is not the fault of those in business. How many of the church's spiritual leaders ever challenged them and helped them understand what Jesus meant by his powerful salt metaphor and how this might relate to them vis-à-vis media and the arts? Christian colleges, even those with media and arts-related majors, apparently have never seen the need to develop and teach business courses related to the media and arts. Evidently they are not interested in challenging their business majors to serve in the area as a reasonable service to God. As a result, we have left creative Christians largely out there to fend for themselves. This is poor stewardship of God's creative gifts. Much of Christian creativity is squandered because there is no Christian business and financial talent to walk alongside. One of the ironies of this situation is that the very few competent Christian business professionals serving in this area do very well financially. There is no reason why high quality Christian endeavors in media and the arts should not be profitable. But we must be willing to make a serious investment in them, artistically, financially, and in business acumen. For the most part, we have not been willing to do this.

If our Christian leaders convened a summit on media and the arts, a very high short term priority would be to challenge Christians with business, legal, and financial resources to begin exercising them in a much more focused and intentional effort to serve the nation and God's kingdom. For the long term, an effort should begin to encourage churches, Christian colleges, universities, and seminaries to inspire, challenge, and equip obedient Christians to consider lives of service as business adjuncts in media and the arts. We should begin to see Christian parents encouraging their children to be business missionaries to America, specializing in facilitating and sponsoring media and the arts. Desperately needed are attorneys, agents, publicists, accountants, financiers, and those who understand all the distribution channels for television programming, movies, art, and literature.

When a Christian writes a brilliant screenplay with great entertainment value and a positive message for the country, there should be someone who would, in a very professional way, see that he or she would be given every possibility of having it produced and distributed. When a Christian movie producer, such as Frank Schroeder, who produced *The Pistol,* has another movie concept, he should have ready access to a pool of investment funds to use in production and distribution in the same way other producers have access to funds put together through investment programs. When a Christian has a well-conceived idea for a television series or special, he or she should know exactly where to take it to have it packaged in a compelling professional way and presented to networks and advertisers. Christian writers with obvious talent and something to say should not have to wonder if their work will ever be read by agents and editors who count, because they know there will be someone to represent and publish the work. When Christian visual artists put together significant bodies of work, they should never have to worry about whether that work will be displayed, marketed, and distributed. Obviously, we are such a long way from this ideal. We need to begin now to understand the need and the vast possibilities.

I have a long-shot dream of a Christian Media and Arts Summit. If this dream ever were to come to fruition, here are some of the people and institutions I, at least, would invite. (The list is alphabetical but not inclusive.)

Bob Abernathy, *Religion and Ethics Newsweekly*

Roberta Ahmanson, philanthropist

The Amy Foundation (the Church Writing Group Movement)

Leith Anderson, pastor and author

Robert C. Andriya, the Council for Christian Colleges and Universities

Asbury College Department of Radio and Television

Loren Balman, Word Music

George Barna, pollster

Fred Barnes, *Weekly Standard*

Joe Battaglia, Renaissance Communications

Margaret Becker, recording artist

John D. Beckett, businessman
Rick Bee, Biola University
The Big Idea Co. (Veggie Tales)
Bill Bippes, professor of art
Pat Boone, entertainer and producer
Bill Bright, Campus Crusade for Christ
Harold O. J. Brown, Center on Religion and Society, Rockford Institute
William F. Buckley, *National Review*
Bob Buford, cable television entrepreneur
Howard E. Butt, Jr., businessman
Lou Carlozo, *Chicago Tribune*
Dan Cathy, businessman
CIVA
Charles Colson, Prison Fellowship
Jim Cymbala, pastor and author
Frank DeFord, *Newsweek*
Donald Dell, ProServ, Inc.
Jimmy Draper, LifeWay Christian Resources
The Eli Lilly Endowment
The Fieldstand Foundation
John Fischer, writer
Bill and Gloria Gaither, songwriters and performers
George Gallup, pollster
Gaylord Communications
J. Philip Glasgow, Christian Comedy College
Billy Goodwin, recording artist
Len Goss, Broadman & Holman Publishers
Amy Grant, recording artist
Max Greiner, sculptor
Os Guinness, Trinity Forum
Johnny Hart, cartoonist
Jody Hassett, CNN
Billy Ray Hearn, music impresario

William Arthur Herring, painter
Hugh Hewitt, PBS Producer
Inter Mission of Hollywood Presbyterian Church
Paul and Nicole Johnson, actors, speakers, and writers
Mark Joseph—MJM
Neal Joseph, *crosswalk.com*
Kenneth S. Kantzer, Trinity International University
Jack Kemp, former congressman
Darlene Koldenhoven, vocalist and songwriter
Barry Landis, Atlantic Records
Terry Lindvall, CBN
Roland Lundy, Idea Entertainment
Terry Mattingly, Scripps-Howard and Regent University
Bill Mattox, *USA Today*
Michael Maudlin, *Christianity Today*
Media Fellowship International
Ava Memmen, the Heartland Film Festival
Moody Bible Institute Radio Department
Ken Myers, Mars Hill Audio
Norm Miller, Interstate Batteries and movie producer
Norman Miller, music impresario
Bill Murchison, *Dallas Morning News*
Richard John Neuhaus, *First Things*
Scott Nolte, Taproot Theatre
David Pack, musician
David Palmer, Squint Entertainment
Bill Parker, *crosswalk.com*
Bad Paxson, PAX television network
Charlie Peacock, musician, recording artist, record
　producer, songwriter
Stephen Pendergast, Squint Entertainment
Larry Poland, Master Media
Bill Romanowski, Calvin College
Michael Rosebush, Focus on the Family

Jeff Sagansky, PAX
Frank Schroeder, movie producer
Quentin J. Schultze, Calvin College
Michael W. Smith, entertainer
Dennis Spencer, SFX Sports Group
Peter Steinfels, *New York Times*
John Styll, CCM Communications
Steve Taylor, Squint Entertainment
The Templeton Foundation
Cal Thomas, *Los Angeles Times*
Vision Quest
Ken Wales, movie and television producer
Michael Warren, television producer
Peggy Wehmeyer, ABC News
Martha Williamson, television producer
Worldwide Pictures (Billy Graham Evangelistic
    Association)
Sealy Yates, Yates and Yates Agency
Wes Yoder, The Ambassador Agency
Young Life

Whether anything anything is ever as grandiose as my dream Christian Media and Arts Summit, the point is that every individual Christian has a responsibility to the country and, more importantly, to scriptural obedience as it relates to being salt in our society. As I have said, this is one of the universal imperatives of Scripture in the same way that proclaiming the gospel and making disciples is commanded for every Christian. This is true if you live in a small Midwestern town, as I do, or in one of the media capitols of the nation. It is true if you are a media mogul yourself, or a housewife or factory worker. If you are a Christian, you are called to be salt. Being salt can't be casual or cavalier. It can't be hit or miss, irregular or spasmodic. Real obedience requires a regular, systematic, and

very intentional commitment to each of the three imperatives. We are not necessarily called to be successful, or
even influential. We are called to be faithful. Be sure to
include some element of community salting as a part of
your walk of faith, and you will gain the joy that always
comes with obedience.

I hope your church will provide some structure for you
to begin or expand your service in this area. Among the
very best programs available to churches is the Church
Writing Group Movement, which assists church members
interested in using their local newspaper to convey messages of righteousness. They provide wonderful materials,
along with a regular newsletter, to instruct and encourage
those who want to compose positive, Scripture-laced letters to the editor, op-ed pieces, and special articles with
Christian themes.[10] Some of the ways local churches are
helping members to be faithful include public displays of
art by Christians, Christian film festivals with an emphasis on inviting those outside the church, and Christian
music concerts, again with an emphasis on taking the
music and its message to those outside the church. If your
own church is not up to speed, talk with your pastor and
get something going. If that doesn't work, do your own
thing. This might be as simple as regularly, prayerfully
introducing scriptural considerations into the conversation at your barber or beauty shop, or as complex as
organizing a group of Christian friends to call in regularly
to local radio talk shows with a very congenial question
or comment from a Christian perspective. The point is not
so much what you do, although you certainly want to do
positive and productive things, but that you do something
in service to your community and in obedience to Christ.
The vast majority of Christians never do anything like
this, and our communities reflect it.

It is very important to remember that being salt is almost never a negative activity. It is not about protests, petitions and boycotts. It is not about criticizing and negative critiques. It is about lovingly, prayerfully introducing biblical alternatives and ways of thinking. It is, as has been said before, about preparing the way for the ultimate message of the gospel. It is certainly not about whining about how bad things are. For most Christians to complain about television, for example, is hardly even intellectually honest. The huge number of Christians in America could easily change the face of prime-time television simply by using our remote controls in a much more thoughtful way. We do this in a positive way by our support of shows such as *Touched by an Angel* and *Promised Land.* They are on the air because we watch them, and for no other reason. This is exactly the reason *NYPD Blue* and all the other raunchy sitcoms are on—because we watch them. If all the people who tell the pollsters they are Christians refused to watch the raunch, those shows would be off the air in short order and the networks would have to scramble to find replacement programming.

The dilemma is illustrated within my own family. Our younger daughter, Lynn, the schoolteacher in Dallas, is a godly young lady deeply involved in her church and a very serious student of the Bible in Bible Study Fellowship and Kay Arthur's Precepts. Yet Lynn watches *Ally McBeal,* one of the most decadent shows on television! (How about it Lynn? How about tuning out the trash TV and tuning in to something better?)

Whenever Christian leaders, especially pastors with a broadcast platform, blame anyone other than Christians themselves for bad television, there is a strong element of intellectual dishonesty present. Christians watch the worst stuff on television and produce only a bare minimum of quality television as an alternative. We need for our leaders to stop wasting airtime, print space, and money complaining about television and blaming others for it. This will never lead toward quality viewing. They need to help encourage and facilitate the production of quality programming. As I have said elsewhere, if the Christian whiners, complainers, and blamers had their way, the best that would happen to America's television screens is that they would fade to black. There would be nothing on the air. It is always much easier to complain and blame than it is to do the terribly difficult work of providing quality alternatives and exercising viewing discipline. The lack of viewing discipline is terribly hard to defend these days, given the huge variety of options available via broadcast, cable, and satellite. There are also more and more quality videos available. You can always pop a *Veggie Tales* video into your VCR!

As PAX TV, the new network currently consisting of more than eighty stations, continues to build, both of those running it, Christian Bud Paxson and observant Jew Jeff Sagansky, as well as Christians and religious Jews in the television audience throughout America, will have exciting opportunities and daunting challenges. The stakes for the country are very significant. Paxson and Sagansky are both very knowledgeable and experienced television executives. Sagansky knows prime-time programming extremely well, given his long string at CBS.

The challenge for the religious community in the country will be to support the network while it is building and beyond. At the same time, it should be held to a very high standard. The strategy of filling its prime-time schedule with old off-network reruns during its early months and years is probably a good one. In the long run, however, the great potential of PAX will either be realized or unrealized by how well it develops or acquires original programming to meet the needs of a diverse nationwide audience of all ages. In other words, will it become a real network? Because running old shows is almost risk free and guaranteed to be profitable, Paxson and Sagansky will have to fight the temptation to take the easy way out, like Pat Robertson did with his Family Channel, putting the network on autopilot and sitting back to make a lot of money. They can do that, but they will then be vastly underserving Christians and other Americans.

PAX also needs to be very vigilant to see that it does not begin looking like what is commonly known as "Christian Television" in America. Embarrassingly, so-called Christian television is characterized by bad signals, bad production, bad lighting, bad audio, bad graphics, bad suits, bad haircuts, bad hair pieces, bad English, and bad theology. The average American television viewer can spot a "Christian" television program at the flick of a remote control button and wisely zaps it as fast as his or her thumb can move. This kind of television is worse than no television at all. It contributes to the idea that Christians are all incompetent boobs and boors interested only in stupid chatter. Too often PAX still looks too much like those programs. The PAX "environment" for even the better produced shows sometimes sends a negative message. For example, The Big Idea Co. produced a brilliant *Veggie Tales* animated Christmas special for PAX, but the programming around it and the integration of commercial messages in it was definitely not up to "real" network standards. The well-produced, enjoyable and timely Christian music concerts on PAX are seriously marred by the constant repetition of the same cheesy, low-budget commercials over and over. The network needs to significantly strengthen its "standards and practices" rules in this regard. Commercials and their placement need to meet a higher and more professional standard. In the long run, it will be better to give commercial spots to Coca-

Cola, Gillette, the automobile companies, and other quality advertisers than to run the same poorly produced spots ad infinitum. If the network delivers the audience it should, the major advertisers will come along as paying customers, and PAX will not look like one of those cheesy and sleazy "Christian" networks.

PAX TV, whether Paxson and Sagansky plan it or like it, will be the flagship network for spiritual people in television, and it will largely define what it means to be religiously serious for many Americans. Given the deplorable way the faith is currently represented by networks and stations using the name Christian, PAX has a daunting task. Christians should pray for those in charge. They should be supportive and encouraging viewers, and say thanks for the good things they do and show. We should ask them to do better when they do less than their best. Christian television producers should be taking a constant stream of quality programs and programming ideas to them without in any way neglecting the more established networks.

My hope and prayer is that Christians in America will need to apologize less and less for neglecting media, entertainment, and the arts as a means for letting the nation know who we are and whom we serve. A "wide door of effective service" is open to us. The "adversaries" are mostly our own lack of vision and commitment. We can do so much better.

CHAPTER 6

Public Relations: Substance and Perception

CHRISTIANS IN AMERICA HAVE HUGE PUBLIC RELATIONS problems, and most of them are of our own making. Whether the problems are of our own making or not, they must be addressed in the most energetic, systematic, and cogent way possible. Our ability to serve our country and effectively to build God's kingdom depends on how well we deal with both substance and perception. To the extent we cannot overcome at least some of the negative stereotypes in at least some of the minds of thinking Americans, our effectiveness to serve will be hampered. Few are going to accept offers of truth from those they believe to be haters, racist, antiintellectual, out of touch with reality, sexist, hypocritical, or self-righteous. As unfair as these perceptions are, they are all very real public relations problems for Christians and the church in America today.

Serious Christians in this country will never be "popular." Popularity is not and should not be our goal. The Bible is very clear that neither our message nor our Savior will ever be universally accepted, and The Way will always be maligned to some extent. For the right reasons, it is OK if we are rejected and maligned. Even if we have represented and presented the truth of the gospel and the beauty of Christ in the best possible way and, to the extent we are able, lived out both in our lives, many will still mock and scoff. That will never change. The long and the short of it is that we need to be obedient, and then God will bring those he wills to accept and embrace the truth. But when we fail in our obedience and when we fail to counter misconceptions and misperceptions about the message and about Christ, huge problems ensue, and our effective service is significantly retarded.

The only effective public relations are quality personal relations. We can overcome some, but not all, of our public relations problems by practicing the very best personal relations possible. In this regard we need a return to what American Christians in an earlier day called "careful living." Careful living is about doing everything right or making things right when we don't. Christians in an earlier era were known as the kind of people who walked several miles to return even a penny given to them as too much change from a purchase. They were regarded as the kind of people who could not sleep if they had left a misconception or an argument with someone. Careful living by many more individual Christians would significantly lessen our massive public relations problems. What would happen if more of us were to be sure to do what we say we will do, say thanks early and often, and if we apologized quickly when warranted? What would happen if we did the best job possible whatever it might be and were responsive to others in a consistent and timely way? What would happen is that the nation at large would have a much harder time believing many of the bad things about us they now certainly do believe. What would happen is that we could serve more effectively.

Careful living still exists among American Christians. I was treated to a very wonderful example of it recently while visiting Dallas. I went to hear O. S. Hawkins preach at the historic First Baptist Church. In his message, he quoted a lady, and the quotes did not cast her in a very favorable light. Some days after I returned home to Illinois, I received a letter from Hawkins, evidently sent to everyone he could track down in that huge congregation. In that letter he said he had since learned the quotes he had been given (apparently he had not done his own research) were not accurate and that the woman had not said the things he attributed to her. That is careful Christian living! May it set an example for all of us, including me. If Christians in America could more and more return to careful living, we would still need to mount a well-thought-out and continuous public relations campaign in order to perform our service to America more effectively. But we would start from a much-advanced position.

In our day, public relations and publicity have been given a bad image. We tend to think of both only in terms of hype and spin. The spin-doctors of politics and commerce have given them an undeservedly bad reputation. This is unfortunate because both are perfectly legitimate and even necessary pursuits. And they are necessary in the effective promotion of the gospel message and the church. We need more Christians pursuing public relations and publicity, and we only need to look to the life and times of Jesus to see how he used them to such great effect.

John the Baptist was the best prepared, most carefully selected advance man of all time. Actually, he was conceived and born for the job. John set a high standard for the profession of public relations and publicity even then that we still need to follow. For example, his timing was impeccable. This is an important prerequisite for success in public relations. Christians have rarely been organized and ready to seize the moment. When occasions in our national life have literally begged for a Christian response, too often we have been silent. I couldn't help but be struck by the almost total lack of a Christian response to the horrible and tragic high school shootings in Littleton, Colorado. Almost everyone else was weighing in with opinions, but there seemed to be an almost eerie silence coming from the evangelical church. The nation needed to hear Christian comfort and concern, and to be offered a Christian solution going beyond more metal detectors and additional campus police.

In order to make effective offers of biblical truth at times of national tragedy and triumph, it is necessary to be known to the producers of the national news shows, television magazine programs, newsmagazines, and to the editors of the major daily newspapers. They need to have access to Christians listed in their Rolodexes, people they know are reliable sources of cogent, succinct, articulate Christian comment. During the national coverage of the Littleton shooting, one could almost feel the producers desperately scrambling to find someone, anyone who would have something meaningful to say. Evidently, from what I saw, the larger broadcast networks didn't find anyone with anything to say from a biblical perspective. Franklin Graham did a wonderful job on *Larry King Live* before the much smaller CNN audience. He was able to do this because he and his father had already positioned themselves with King and his producers. We cannot expect Graham or a small handful of others to carry the whole load in the future. We need to position ourselves better in order to serve better. Our timing must be better.

Another standard set by John the Baptist for contemporary publicity and public relations is adherence at all times to absolute truth. Truth must always be the standard. John gave good news and bad; he told the truth. Christians have not always been willing to do this. Waffling on the truth has been so common that there is even a phrase used in our subculture when Christians are fudging or embellishing the truth—"evangelistically speaking." Let me pick on my own small denomination in this regard. It is in serious decline and shrinking in absolute numbers, yet all the denominational publications make it seem the denomination is flourishing. This is speaking "evangelistically" and does not measure up to John's standard of absolute truth. Of all people, Christians need to tell the truth.

About Jesus, John said, "He must become greater; I must become less" (John 3:30). This should be the motto of everyone representing the Lord Jesus. He is the client. The representative, or agent, should never attempt to overshadow the client. Some of the so-called televangelists who dominate the television airwaves need to reread the John 3:30 text. John the Baptist was a great publicity and public relations man who teaches us about timing, the absolute standard of truth, and, most importantly, about the necessity that all our efforts be aimed at promoting not ourselves or our organizations but Jesus Christ and his gospel. Timing, truth, and the person of Jesus should be the watchwords of publicity and public relations that are Christian. If we would practice these at all times, the nation would benefit.

It should come as no surprise that Jesus himself was a master of publicity and public relations. The gospel accounts of his earthly ministry show how he used these techniques to such great effect. There were times Jesus told people to be silent about the things they witnessed him doing, and there were other times he told them to tell everyone. This goes to timing. In one of the famous uses of publicity and public relations, Jesus told the former Gadarene demoniac (Mark 5:1-15), whom he had healed, not to go with him, but to stay and tell everyone in the surrounding ten cities what had been done for him. Jesus returned some time later to find the area a very fruitful one for his ministry. Timing and a good, enthusiastic, truthful PR man had proven highly effective. Jesus also used polling, one of the essential tools of publicity and public relations. He asked, for example, "Who do people say that I am?" He wanted to know how his message was "playing." Christians need to do the same thing today. We need to know how we are doing in the eyes of the people we are trying to serve. The message should never be changed to accommodate the poll numbers, in the manner of reckless politicians, but the numbers should be used to help with strategy and tactics.

Remembering that the first public relations and publicity goal of Christians is to promote Christ and the gospel, we need to do a much better job of having our good deeds reflect credit on him. There is no question that Christians do a huge amount of good in this country. But somehow, Jesus does not get much of the credit for it. Both the average guy on the street and the media elite seem not to equate all that is done for Christ's sake with Jesus and the gospel. We provide homeless shelters, soup kitchens, clothing drives, day-care centers, battered women's homes, hospitals, crisis pregnancy centers, work on Native American reservations, and work in Appalachia and in many other parts of the country. Even though this kind of charity happens only because of the committed church, voluntarily funded entirely by committed Christians, no credit is really given to the One who motivates it all. That is the fault of Christians.

Jesus said, "Let your light shine before men, that they may see your good deeds and praise your Father in heaven" (Matt. 5:16). I believe the light about which this Scripture speaks is good publicity and public relations, the sort that make sure the good deeds do indeed glorify our heavenly Father. Good deeds are never enough in and of themselves. In fact, Scripture calls them "filthy rags" if not done to honor God. Over the past several years, we have begun for some reason to shy away from allowing the motives for our good deeds to be known. We are shy about saying, "We are doing this for you in the name of Jesus," or, "This is being given to you because Jesus has given so much to us." We fail to leverage (in the very best sense of that word) our good deeds for the sake of the gospel. Our obvious and overt good deeds do not help much to ameliorate the generally bad reputation we have in much of society. It doesn't matter too much whether this is fair. No one promised fairness. The point is that we need to do better in the way we let our light shine boldly and tactfully to let people know that it shines for Jesus' sake.

The Salvation Army is possibly instructive on this. The Army does a tremendous amount of good in this country. I happen to know that the leaders of the Salvation Army could not be more sincere and dedicated Christians, doing all they do for the sake of the Lord Jesus. In the eyes of most Americans, however, the Army is seen as a good organization exactly like the United Way is seen as a good organization. In an effort to be inclusive and to be sure that major donors are not offended, organizations such as the Salvation Army and Habitat for Humanity water down and sometimes even mask their true Christian motivation. Maybe this is good fund-raising strategy. But is it good kingdom strategy? Not if the gospel suffers and not if the nation suffers. We need to do a much better job of seeing the good things that Christians do for the sake of the gospel actually reflect favorably on the gospel and on sincere Christians. This is good public relations.

On March 31, 1998, the *Wall Street Journal* ran a piece on its editorial page headlined "The Minister of Defense Meant No Offense." It was written by Andrew Peyton Thomas, a Phoenix attorney, and was in defense of football great Reggie White. White's comments before the Wisconsin State Assembly less than a week before brought down a firestorm against the godly, recently retired Green Bay Packer great (who is also a minister of the gospel). White's pro-God, antihomosexual, anti-lying-in-the-White House message was roundly and deliberately misinterpreted by the national press, most of which was generated by homosexuals. Thomas's was a wonderful piece of Christian public relations. The article was beautifully written and, best of all, was timely. The *WSJ* article very cogently and persuasively made the case that White's comments were "controversial only insofar as the Bible is controversial." It was a great job. But even with the massive circulation of the *Wall Street Journal*, the article could not come close to countering all the unfair and negative nationwide publicity the comments generated.

More than a year later the Associated Press ran a story about the cancellation of a prison ministry fund-raiser at which Reggie White was supposed to speak. According to the director of The Philadelphians Ministry, the public response to White's speaking at the event was "very negative." It is hard to imagine a ministry event not being an unqualified success when an all-time great and certain

NFL Hall of Fame entrant was to speak. But evidently this ministry thought that would be the case. White is a wonderful man and a very dedicated Christian, but in the short term his ministry will be less than it might be, due to these unfair reactions. This is bad public relations result when our light fails to shine.

In the summer of 1998, the Southern Baptist Convention, America's largest Protestant denomination, held its annual convention in Salt Lake City. For weeks prior to the massive event, almost all publicity focused on the Baptist's decision to hold their event in the Mormon stronghold. It was typically seen as a sort of "in your face" move. Mormonism and the straight biblical doctrine of the SBC could hardly be further apart. But during and after the convention, almost all the publicity was directed at just one comment issued from the convention relating to the submission of wives to their husbands (a concept that comes not from the Baptists but from the Bible in Eph. 5:22). Anti-Christian feminists went berserk and had a field day, aided of course by much of the nation's press.

Afterwards, I read and heard many brilliant explanations from Baptists and other Christians about the reasonableness and the efficacy of the teaching on wives submitting themselves to their husbands. There is no question that this teaching represents biblical truth. But to expect non-Christians, who have no idea what it means and requires of husbands and wives to understand and embrace it, is to live in fantasyland.

In my book *Deadly Detours*, I quoted Ron Sider as follows:

> Few things are more important today than a return to biblical principles and practice in the area of sexuality and the family. Tragically, Christian people who do not know what the Bible teaches too often employ harsh rhetoric and engage in nasty culture wars in a way that repels those who most need to hear our message. They will never listen if they

think we hate them. But think of how powerful a different
kind of servant witness and wholesome modeling would be.
Think of the impact if the first thing radical feminists thought
of when the conversation turned to evangelical men was that
they had the best reputation for keeping their marriage vows
and serving their wives in the costly fashion of Jesus at the
cross. Think of the impact if the first thing the homosexual
community thought of when someone mentioned evangelicals
was that they were the people who lovingly ran the AIDS
shelters and tenderly cared for them down to the last gasp. A
little consistent wholesome modeling and costly servanthood
are worth millions of true words harshly spoken.[11]

This is not at all to say that Reggie White's words in
front of the Wisconsin State Assembly or those of the
Southern Baptists in Salt Lake City were either harshly
spoken or biblically uninformed. They definitely were not,
and I am absolutely sure they were intended for good.
Perhaps, however, they were not as informed as they
might have been by the masterly public relations example
set by Jesus. He demonstrated over and over that all the
people are not ready for all the truth at all times. He even
told his own disciples from time to time that they themselves were not ready. It is always a mistake to toss out
complex biblical concepts to a public that hasn't even
accepted the most basic and fundamental of the truths of
the Bible on which these concepts rest. The cynical and
unbelieving shoot the concepts down with clever sound
bites. The result is almost inevitable: most are driven even
further from the heart-changing power of the gospel.

The absolutely true and valid biblical truth that
Christian wives should submit to Christian husbands,
who love, serve, and sacrifice for them the way Christ
did for the Church, should be taught and modeled in all
Christian homes. But we need to use the public relations
techniques taught to us by the Lord Jesus to teach some
of the more basic, more fundamental, more easily
understood truths. Such truths include the fact that

there is a loving God who has spoken to us through his Word and who has revealed himself through his Son. Those who become convinced of these more basic Christian truths can then be taught about wives submitting to their husbands.

Before most gays and lesbians ever realize the practice of homosexuality is wrong, they will need to be convinced that God loves them and that Christians also love them. This message needs to be conveyed on a priority basis. It is a much more important and more vital message than the (also absolutely true) message that homosexual practices are bad.

Truth, timing, and Jesus need to be the watchwords of a much more vigorous, concerted, and ongoing public relations campaign by Christians and Christian organizations if we are ever going to have the proper platform to serve in the best possible way. While there doesn't need to be a big monolithic "one voice" campaign, we do need tens of thousands of individual Christians to emulate Andrew Peyton Thomas, the Phoenix attorney who weighed in to support his Christian brother Reggie White when White needed it. They do not need to be skilled and erudite, just willing to write letters to their local papers in these kinds of situations. And remember: truth, timing, and Jesus. These letters must tell biblical truth, must be as timely as possible, and must always draw people to Jesus and his gospel. They should never be used to try to score points on abortion, gun control, prayer in schools, or any of the other causes that captivate so many Christians and are usually so divisive. Truth, timing, and Jesus: This is the way to begin to face our public relations dilemma.

Some churches should have an advertising campaign, always at the ready, to initiate at exactly the right moment—not to build attendance, but to build truth. An advertisement that said something like, "Christians do not hate homosexuals or anyone else," would have been very timely and appropriate in the wake of the awful beating death of the young gay college student in Wyoming at a time when many were trying to blame Christians. Of course, some claiming to be Christians and to represent Christian thinking contributed to this horrible state of affairs by the signs they carried and the ungodly way they acted at the funeral and other events surrounding the awful event. We desperately need truthful publicity and public relations to counteract these untrue and damaging representations of Christians and the church. Truth, timing, and Jesus need to be the watchwords and the motivation of sincere Christians.

Of all the public relations problems faced by Christians, perhaps the biggest one relates in fact to homosexuals. We have done such a poor and inconsistent job of letting the rest of the nation know what the Bible really says about homosexuals and homosexuality that far too few people, including most homosexuals, really understand a biblically consistent view on this topic. We have done an even poorer job of demonstrating that view. The results have been tragic. The country at large and homosexuals in particular honestly feel that we Christians hate gays. They are owed a deep apology. Here are just some of the truths we need to be communicating on this matter, and we need to be doing this the best way we know how:

1. Homosexuals are people for whom Christ died.
2. Homosexuals deserve the opportunity to consider the claims of Christ, and these claims should be presented to them in a clear loving way, the same way we would communicate them to anyone else.
3. Homosexual acts are sinful and cannot be condoned, but in eternal terms are no more sinful than

any other sinful act. Sin of any kind must be forgiven, and any sin that is not forgiven is utterly vile to a holy God.

4. How people become homosexuals may be of academic interest, but it is no more central to the work of the church where homosexuals are concerned than how heterosexuals become lustful or how thieves become covetous.

5. The number of Americans who are homosexuals, whether 1 percent or 10 percent of the population, is an interesting sociological and demographic question. But it shouldn't have any more to do with the work of the church than the percentage of car thieves, spouse abusers, or adulterers in the United States.

6. The question of whether or not AIDS is God's judgment on homosexuals is in no way central to the work of the church where homosexuals and AIDS victims are concerned. Without in any way insulting homosexuals, it is worth noting that Jesus seemed to have no interest in the origins of leprosy, but only in helping and healing it.

7. As responsible parents, citizens, and Christians, we need to be concerned about our public schools, about fairness for all our fellow citizens, about our military, and about all the other components of a democratic society.

As Christians, our first allegiance is to our Lord Jesus Christ and his kingdom. If we consistently integrate our faith into all of life and do a much better job of communicating this to the country as a whole, our fellow citizens will not see nearly as much conflict between what the Bible teaches and the way we live. But we must be ready with truth, timing and Jesus. When the haters march under Christian banners proclaiming utterly false and demonic doctrines of violence and hate, Bible-believing Christians must do a much better job of responding with truth, timing, and Jesus. If we don't, we will continue to fail the country in a very profound way.

While we must do much better in the public relations arena to validate what we do there, we also must do a much better job on the ground where the real end games of the work of Christ and his kingdom are always played out. Some questions I have posed in this regard appeared in an earlier book.

Is it not ironic and does it not seem strange that American Christians can engage with such enthusiasm for ministries to former enemies (The USSR) thousands of miles away. Is it not ironic and does it not seem strange that we support a ministry to convicted criminals guilty of every kind of crime from mass murder, to rape, to child molestation, to all kinds of white collar crimes? Yet, we have almost no enthusiasm for ministering to a group of people who live with us and work with us but who are not only dying in their sins by the thousands every week but also, while they live, are existing in a kind of surreal world that is a foretaste of the hell to which the church is assigning them. . . .

Where are the great evangelical leaders? Where are the evangelical denominations? Where are the highly organized parachurch organizations? Where are the Co-Mission type efforts to present Jesus in all his beauty, majesty, power, glory and compassion to homosexuals? Where is the Chuck Colson to lead an effort to reach this poor, needy and dying group of people?[12]

I do not mean to denigrate the wonderful organizations that are working very valiantly in this effort. They are real heroes. They are, however, mostly underrecognized, underfunded, and underappreciated. They are very worthy of your participation, prayer, and financial support. Until the Christian church in America begins to do a more credible job in the air (public relations) and on the ground (a direct and consistent reaching out to homosexuals in a biblically consistent way), our message to America will continue to be seen as flawed and compromised. We must do better.

One thing I think could help is for every Christian to have a copy of a wonderful letter written by the late Richard Halverson. When he wrote this, he was the chaplain of the United States Senate. Halverson wrote:

Dear Friend:

Through the years as a pastor of four churches (in Missouri, California and Maryland), *it was my responsibility (and privilege) to minister to those who were homosexual.*

Based on this experience, let me share *how I would respond to a child of mine* who discovered that he/she was homosexual . . .

First, and most importantly, *I would not cease loving them*, or love them less than before they shared their situation with me.

As a matter of fact, I would *love them more than ever*, if that were possible.

They would have my hearing—*as often and as long as they wanted to discuss the matter* with me.

I would do my best *not to be judgmental*!

I would not treat them as "queer" or whatever other designation is a "put down."

I would do all I could to *persuade them* to be chaste (just as I would a heterosexual child before marriage).

I would remind them with all the wisdom God gives me, *that He loves them*, that *He understands them*, that *His love is unconditional and everlasting.*

I would urge their *total commitment to Jesus Christ*, that He might change them—as He transformed my life from pleasure loving playboy, and as He transformed many others to be His obedient servants—to conform to His perfect plan for their lives.

I would do all in my power—and with love—*to try and dissuade them from adopting a homosexual life-style.*

I would remind them that Christ created them for Himself, and they could become themselves, only as they gave themselves to Him that He might rule in their bodies. (Colossians 1:16, 27–29; 2:9–10; Romans 12:1–2). "Know ye not that your body is the temple of the Holy Spirit ?" (I Corinthians 6:19).

Grace and Peace
Richard C. Halverson[13]

To me, Halverson's sentiment expresses it all. While this wonderful letter deals specifically with a parent-child relationship, its truths are so universal that it can be applied to every Christian's relationship with every nonbelieving homosexual, and it can help to inform every statement Christians make about homosexuals and homosexuality. I wish every Christian shared Dr. Halverson's principles. Every time we get an opportunity to speak out or respond to questions about Christianity vis-à-vis homosexuality, it would be good to reread the letter.

Among the most pernicious and damaging public relations problems faced by American Christians is the perception among many that we are racists. If there are those among us who actually are racists, it needs to be said first of all that there is absolutely no scriptural basis for any sort or any degree of racism in the Christian faith. Anyone practicing or believing in any type of racism is either ignoring Scripture or being willfully disobedient to it. This is a message we need to convey much more regularly, forcefully, and convincingly to the church and the country.

All Americans need to know that when they see acts of or hear expressions of racism parading under a Christian banner, or done, supposedly, to advance the church, that these are in no way, shape, or form Christian. In fact, they are antithetical to every tenet of Christianity. Passivity by Christians in the face of public racist expressions in the name of our faith will not suffice. Public, well-publicized racist acts and expressions must be countered by well-publicized repudiations. It is not necessary or advisable to attack individuals or groups, but it is very necessary to attack false and evil ideas.

Promise Keepers did a great deal toward bringing the problem of racism to the forefront of thinking among Christian men. Unfortunately, many felt their antiracism message became distorted and diluted by an unscriptural and unnecessary concentration on the historical sins of racism. We neither bear the responsibility for nor can we atone for what others did before we were born. We have more than enough to handle making sure that all Americans know the glorious gospel of Jesus Christ does not condone racism of any variety, and we then need to be very sure that none is practiced in our personal lives or in our churches.

This is a message for both black and white Christians, and for Christians of all ethnic and racial origins. We must work much harder and much smarter to be sure that all Americans understand the real unity we have in Christ.

Any thought by other Americans that Christians are racists is terrible, but the thought that Christians could be anti-Semites is particularly intolerable. Christians and Jews have so much in common and share so many common goals that it is absolutely vital that Christians never allow themselves to be seen as anything other than people who honor God's covenant people. We need to be making common cause with them as we join observant Jews in the effort to instill as much righteousness as possible into American society. Wonderful examples of this are the way Christians have befriended distinguished film critic Michael Medved, an observant Jew. Some of his books have been published in the Christian orbit, and he has spoken to many different Christian groups. (Christians, who number many times more than Jews in America, have not produced even a single film critic with the stature and standing of Michael Medved.) To help articulate our Judeo-Christian message to and about Hollywood, the aforementioned Jeff Sagansky, also an observant Jew, has joined the PAX network. We need many more examples of Jews and Christians working together to better America. And Christians need to be much more vigilant and forceful in repudiating any acts or messages even hinting that Christians are anti-Semitic.

The public relations problem Christians have with abortion is almost the same kind as that we have with homosexuals. And it needs to be combated in much the same way. Our absolutely justified, total revulsion at the abomination of abortion has been allowed to be played out in the nation's media in such a way as to depict Christians as violent and hate filled. As with our relationship to homosexuals, we have allowed the very public and even violent and murderous actions of a relatively few people, claiming to be Christians, to sully our faith in the eyes of America. And while we have done some better "on the ground" work as far as serving those who need us so desperately, in the whole area of the abortion disaster, we have not done nearly enough and do not have nearly the story to tell we should have. I certainly want to laud the fantastic and heroic work of the Crisis Pregnancy Centers and similar organizations, as well as that of adoption agencies and adoptive parents. Still, we have a very hard time answering some of the questions our opponents hurl at us. The toughest one might be why, on our way to mount protests at abortion clinics, do we drive by thousands of kids who have been born and who desperately need help, and yet we don't stop to help them?

Being a kid in America has never been harder or more dangerous. Never have they needed the gospel more. Until we can be sure that we as the church are doing all we possibly can for children, and being sure that Jesus and his gospel get all the credit for what we do, we will continue to have a massive public relations problem relative to the issue of abortion. This will have a negative effect on our service to America. This in no way means we should ever become complacent about the unmitigated horror of abortion in America. Never! But we must work against it in the most productive way possible, and in the way that will promote and not retard the potential for the gospel to work in the hearts of all Americans.

We must be very sure that every time there are anti-abortion expressions of violence, hate, and murder, with even a hint reflecting anything Christian, they will be met not with a tiny muted voice but with a massive and unified voice of protest. This voice must come from every possible venue and from every possible Christian, especially Christian leaders expressing sorrow and anguish that any of these things could be perpetrated in the name of Christ.

As in other areas in which Christians work so valiantly and give so generously, we must do a better job of publicity and public relations in these areas of homosexuality, racism, anti-Semitism, and abortion. This is not to be done for self-aggrandizement or to promote any particular organization, as I have said before, but for the sake of the gospel, seeing that our good works glorify our Father in heaven.

As I have tried already to stress, for Christians to be at our effective best for our country, we must not be perceived by other Americans as rubes, boors, or out of touch with reality. Certainly, there will always be those who see any element of religious belief and faith as irrational, anti-intellectual, and irrelevant. We can handle this. Whether or not everyone admits it, faith plays such a large part in every person's life. It can be shown to be a very understandable part of a Christian worldview that is consistent and intellectually defensible. But even when laid out systematically, logically, and completely, there will be those who will not accept and adopt Christianity. Again, this is something we can accept. We wish everyone could and would believe the claims of Christ and reap the enormous benefits of this, both in this life and in eternity. Sadly, we know this will not happen. It is much sadder, however, when, by the actions of some Christians, others see our faith as inherently irrational and intellectually indefensible. When we allow ourselves to get caught up in causes which, in and of themselves, are not consistent with what we really believe and are rightfully seen by other thinking Americans as nonsensical, we create massive public relations problems for ourselves and for our faith. These are problems neither Christians nor other Americans need. When they occur, they are problems that must be addressed by thinking and caring believers.

I think the most glaring example of this phenomenon is the prayer in public schools controversy. On the surface, it would seem that every Christian should join wholeheartedly in the campaign to restore prayer to our public schools. The problem is, in my view, this cause will not pass either scriptural or intellectual muster (which should always be compatible), and Americans with any degree of discernment know this. For them to see Christians sucked into this effort by self-serving politicians portrays us as nonthinkers and, often, mean-spirited people as well.

It is important to understand that prayer in public schools has never been banned, and of course it never could be banned. Hundreds of thousands of students pray silently and reverently in public schools every day, and no one tries to stop them. Perhaps millions pray at exam time! The only kind of prayer that is banned is formal, oratorical prayer, the very kind of public prayer that the Bible and Jesus himself denigrated. Why would evangelicals want to go to war over that?

In an increasingly pluralistic, racially and ethnically mixed society such as the United States, legalized public prayer in schools would create huge, untenable problems for Christians and for our effective witness to other Americans. Those who fight so loudly and at such great expense to legalize oratorical prayer in public schools seem to think there is a righteous Christian teacher in every classroom just waiting to be able to begin an effective, fervent prayer ministry with his or her class. Such is far from the case. How would Christian parents react if their elementary child came home and said, "Mommy, today we said a prayer to the Great Spirit that lives in the trees and flowers, and we learned that we are god ourselves. Isn't that neat?" Or, "Today we prayed to the god the boys and girls in India pray to. Tomorrow we get to pray to the god the Japanese boys and girls pray to." This kind of thing is the inevitable outgrowth of legalized school prayer in a pluralistic society. Why do we want to spend our time, money, and effort fighting for this? We shouldn't, and believe me, thinking Americans of goodwill and of all religious persuasions ask the same question.

Except for the will to do so, there is absolutely nothing that prohibits American Christians from bathing our principals, teachers, and students in prayer every day. Certainly our schools, and all those involved with them, need prayer as never before. If Christians are to be able to face other thoughtful Americans in intellectual honesty, we need to stop playing games with this nonissue of legalizing prayer in school and, instead, begin praying regularly and earnestly for our schools. We really should do away with all the florid political and pulpit oratory about legalizing prayer in school and get back to real issues of urgency and concern.

We American Christians have much more important things to do with our time, energy, and money than expend them in frivolous pursuits—even if these pursuits make us feel righteous. We really must begin to take a closer look at our priorities. We need to measure everything we do against what we are uniquely and specifically called to do as followers of Christ. As always, Scripture must point the way. When we allow ourselves to be led into the kind of perilous traps represented by bogus legalization on the school-prayer issue, a number of bad things happen. First, we are distracted from doing the things we are really called and commanded to do. Second, resources of all kinds are simply wasted. Third, we lose our standing with the vast majority of thinking Americans who see us involved with and exercised over such a silly endeavor. They ask, "Why would I want to get involved with that?" When this occurs, we have a much more difficult time communicating the real truth of the gospel, making it harder and harder to serve the country in the way we should. The school-prayer issue presents a massive and delicate public relations problem.

The extent of the problem comes in the need to counter the widespread exposure which, unfortunately, is always given to this kind of thing. It is a delicate problem because we don't want to bash other Christians on this issue, no matter how misguided we think they may be. We need, however, to distance ourselves from bad ideas, and we want to try to do this without distancing ourselves from well-meaning people. This is not easy but must be done. Fortunately, the school-prayer issue and most others of this type, lends itself to a positive kind of response. The most obvious thing we can do is to begin praying more regularly for our schools. We should be sure that our churches are systematically praying for our schools. (How can we organize prayer for our missionaries and not pray for our teachers and students?) We should promote vital and valid prayer ministries focusing on the schools, such as Moms in Touch. Why shouldn't every church have a Moms in Touch chapter? We need to teach through every vehicle open to us the principles of correct prayer, particularly as they relate to schools. Perhaps the most important one is that God is not limited in answering prayers for schools by where the prayer is prayed. In the whole legalization issue, somehow the place of prayer has become more important than prayer itself. God does not care whether prayers for schools are prayed on school property or not.

Why should we care about something God does not care about, especially when it causes so much debilitating and unproductive rancor? I hope Christians by the millions will be sure they are not involved in supporting any of these legalization movements, no matter how well meaning they might sound. Ultimately, they are destructive and counterproductive. Do not send money to those who have made this a cause. Do not show up at their rallies or public protests. Encourage your pastors and church leaders to stay away and to be uninvolved.

As I have tried to show in this chapter, Christians do have some very significant public relations problems. These problems keep us from serving our country and our

Lord as effectively as we should. Inasmuch as Jesus himself has shown us how to use great public relations for the sake of the gospel, we need to follow his perfect example.

CHAPTER 7

The Music of the Spheres

"Music is the soundtrack to the story we're telling through our lives and our communities. Through emotion and word it documents our journey. It looks back at past grace and in gratitude gives God worshipful praise. It looks forward in faith to future grace and gives God praise as well. Music is present when we're born and when we're buried, when we learn our ABCs and when we graduate from high school, when we celebrate birthdays, baptisms, Christmas, and Easter, when we first hear the gospel, when we share our first dance, our first kiss, and when we marry. Music is both a quiet song in our hearts and a thundering symphony that takes our breath away. Our enjoyment of it seems to know no end. It is literally the sonic backdrop to life and culture. All in all, it's possible to say that music is everywhere and not risk exaggeration."

—Charlie Peacock[14]

CHARLIE PEACOCK'S WORDS BEGIN TO GIVE US AN EXCELLENT idea as to the scope and importance of music in our lives. The reality is that music is not only present at the big events of our lives, but actually helps shape the character of those events. It determines, to a large extent, how those events will unfold. The music of our lives will determine how and if we celebrate birthdays, baptisms, Christmas, and Easter. It will also play a large part in how and if we first hear the gospel. With whom we first dance, what kind of dance it will be, and what the dance will mean will, in large measure, be determined by how music has entered our lives up to that point. Music will play a huge part in our first kiss and how that kiss is delivered and received. It will go a long way in determining whom we marry and how the marriage will work. In short, music is an incredibly powerful medium, for good or for ill. It is part of God's created order, and thus, for the church, it is not a luxury but a necessity.

As we enter the new millennium, there is a proliferation of the lists of the "most influential" people in our lives. These lists try to gauge the degree of influence people from all walks of life have had on our society over the last decade or century. Among the ones given the most attention has been the *ABC News* list of the "People of the Century." In the top ten is Elvis Presley. Elvis! Remember, these lists are not necessarily naming people who have only been influential in their fields. Elvis and the Beatles (who are also on many lists) have not only influenced musical style or tastes; they are seen to have a much more significant influence—they have influenced hearts, minds, attitudes, and worldviews.

Music can not only "soothe the savage beast," but it can also create and incite savagery in some. Consider, for example, all the overt violence, the vulgarity, and the almost unbelievably brutal attitude articulated toward women found in some rap music. This music is receiving and deserves to receive close scrutiny. Music is powerful.

Of course, music has been important to people of faith at least since biblical times. It has inspired the Christian church, instructed it, allowed it to worship in most meaningful ways, and provided one of its most effective means of reaching and ministering to those outside the church with the message of the gospel. Now, strangely, music has also become the most divisive of subjects among many Christians, even more divisive than debates over key doctrinal issues.

It is sad but true that more churches in America split over concerns about musical styles in their worship services than over any other consideration. Profound theological questions, preaching effectiveness, quality of evangelistic outreach, Christian education concerns, service to the poor and disadvantaged in the community—all these things take a back seat to disputes among Christians about music! Music and how it is used has surged to the forefront to become topic number one in many churches. Terry Mattingly, religion columnist for Scripps Howard, has said that music is taking such a front seat in the affairs of our churches that many Christians are holding contemporary Christian musicians to a higher standard of conduct than they were expecting even of their own pastors. It may seem astonishing, but in many churches pastors divorce and remarry and remain in the ministry, sometimes at the same church. Hardly an eyebrow is raised. But when musicians Amy Grant and Gary Chapman separated and then divorced, it seemed like multitudes were up in arms. What is going on?

In the Nashville contemporary Christian music community, significant creative marketing and business talent are spent defining what makes a "Christian song," while millions of unchurched and unevangelized music lovers need the best music Christians can create and deliver to them. The Christian-controlled music industry has become very ingrown. We even had the strange spectacle of Michael W. Smith opening the 1998 Dove Awards (Christian music's premiere awards show) telecast with a song, which the powers that be later told him was not eligible to be considered for a Dove Award. It was not sufficiently "Christian" enough, apparently. Give me a break. The storm rages on. America continues to be failed by Christians in the most vital and influential area of Christian music.

Music is such a huge, diverse, and complex subject. Even the most competent music scholars would have to write many volumes to adequately cover the complete field. Generalizations in this area, as in any area, are dangerous and will always be idiosyncratic to some extent. My purpose here, however, is to take a nonscholarly look at how Christians are using or misusing music in serving America and building God's kingdom. I hope to offer some insights on how we can do better.

I love music and have eclectic musical tastes, but I am not a musician or a musician's son. I do have many very close friends among the artists, composers, producers, and record company executives in the business and ministry of contemporary Christian music—or at least I had them before they read this book! Before moving on, though, I want to direct you to two very wonderful books, where you can find much more thorough and scholarly treatments of the theoretical and theological aspects of Christians and music. The first is Charlie Peacock's magnificent book, *At the Crossroads*. The second is Harold Best's wonderful *Music Through the Eyes of Faith*.[15] I cannot recommend these books too highly.

As important as it is, and as great a spiritual gift as it is, and as much potential as it has for good, music should never become an end in itself. It can become an idol, perhaps more easily than almost anything else. If it is to produce not evil but good, and the maximum amount of good for the country and for God's kingdom, then there must be a plan for it. There must be a dedication to a great purpose. The first and highest purpose must be to glorify God with the most excellent music we can possibly produce. That is a prerequisite, a must. But this is really not enough. Great music that will never be heard is a terrible waste. If the Bible needs to be packaged and distributed to produce maximum effect, then certainly the same is true of music.

To the extent there was ever a grand plan or design for the modern Christian-controlled music business, which has dramatically grown up in and around Nashville, this seemed to be it. By getting together in companies which emulated secular record companies, Christian artists could write music, produce records, and distribute them to an eager market. The Christian bookstores provided ready-made distribution outlets. Larger churches became concert halls, and Christian radio stations were the perfect promotional vehicles. All was well and good and the business flourished.

But as the business flourished, the ministry lagged. As Charlie Peacock has written so eloquently in *At the Crossroads*, there was almost no theological base for any of this, and it just developed sort of helter-skelter. All those involved knew they loved Jesus, and they knew they loved music. So they wrote, performed, and sold music about Jesus for like-minded people. Unfortunately, this developed into a ghetto. It was and of course still is a very formidable and complete ghetto, almost entirely self-contained. It has its own raw materials, means of production, distribution, promotion and publicity apparatus, its own governing body, and even its own awards show. Without any question, it is a real ghetto.

Ghettos have several purposes. The overriding one, it seems to me, is to make the people inside the ghetto more comfortable than they would if they had to be outside the ghetto. This is particularly true of the Christian music ghetto, which makes Christian performers and others working in the industry feel cozy and snug inside a comfortable, protective cocoon. The problem is that Christians are not supposed to be comfortable. We are supposed to be aliens and strangers in the larger world. In many ways we are to seek discomfort, the discomfort of operating in a hostile, foreign milieu. When we ghettoize our talents and gifts for our own comfort and use, we cheat the people we are supposed to serve. Ultimately, this means we cheat ourselves. We never know how good we could be outside the ghetto, and we never know the real joy that comes with obedience to scriptural imperatives.

To help us better understand just how a ghetto works, allow me to refer to an example from sports that I first used in my book *Roaring Lambs*. I think it is still useful. Unless you are a very serious tennis fan, you probably do not remember Jun Kuki and Jan Kamiwasumi. During the decade of the seventies, when tennis was becoming a highly organized, widely televised, and very lucrative sport, Kuki and Kamiwasumi were well-respected, class-act journeymen players on the worldwide circuit. I don't think either of them ever won a major professional tournament, but they played very good tennis and earned a great deal of prize money. Beyond this, they added a lot to the appeal of the circuit.

As you have guessed from their names, Kuki and Kamiwasumi are Japanese. In almost every city on the pro tour, the tournaments attracted a good group of Japanese fans who would come to the events especially to see and root for Kuki and Kamiwasumi. Most tournaments would get an extra shot of publicity because local newspapers would do a feature on the two players from Japan. The tour might be in London, Paris, Sydney, or Chicago, but it was more attractive and more interesting to tennis fans because of the two Japanese players.

Kuki and Kamiwasumi represented their country very well. They were great sportsmen, always respectful of their opponents, as well as of the referees and umpires. They always kept their commitments, showed up on time to play, and played very hard and very well, though, of course, they did not always win. In fact, as I said before, they never won a major international professional tournament. Even so, their fellow players, the tournament promoters, the tennis press, television networks, and tennis fans all were very happy to have Jun Kuki and Jan Kamiwasumi on the tour.

Up to this point, Kuki and Kamiwasumi are the last two Japanese players to have played the world tour. Even though the circuit has grown even bigger and more lucrative, no other Japanese players have ever played. The prize money is now in the tens of millions of endorsement dollars available to the top players. Also, the sport has boomed in Japan. It seems that everyone there either plays or wants to play tennis. It is a big sport on television, and there are huge international tournaments in Tokyo. When former President Bush went to Japan, he played tennis with the Emperor, adding even more glamour and prestige to the sport there. But since the time of Kuki and Kamiwasumi, no Japanese players have ventured out to play against the best players in the world on the international tour. Why?

It is simply because tennis has grown so big in Japan and so lucrative for Japanese players who are encouraged to play only in Japanese tournaments. There is little financial incentive for the best Japanese players to go and fight it out with the best players from all the other countries. As one Japanese player told me, "I can make a million dollars a year and never leave home. Why do I want to fly all over the world to make less money and lose a lot of matches against the Europeans and Americans?"

Obviously, with this kind of attitude, no Japanese player is ever going to win Wimbledon or the U.S. Open, the most coveted prizes in tennis. No player from Japan will ever be ranked number one in the world. Japan will almost certainly never win the Davis Cup, the major international team competition. Even more sadly, no future Kuki or Kamiwasumi will be out there in the great international mix of players, bringing their own very special flavor, adding their own special brilliance and perspective to the sport. Japan virtually has disappeared from tennis. In their small island country, a great deal of tennis is played. They play each other in all kinds of tournaments and in all their own cities. Outside of Japan, however, no one ever knows the results. No one knows the names of any of the players. No one cares.

This pretty well represents the sad picture of the Christian music ghetto. In analyzing the contemporary Christian music ghetto, it is necessary to look from several perspectives: from Scripture, from what it provides the church, and from how if affects the performers and the others involved in keeping the ghetto up and running. Here's an example of one of my friends who chose not to remain in the ghetto but rather chose to engage the culture of music as a Christian.

Steve Taylor and Squint Entertainment

Steve Taylor of Squint Entertainment helped modernize Christian music, transforming it from an often lame, Sunday school version of pop culture to a genre that holds its own with the best of secular music. Along the way, though, Steve found himself bound alternately by the expectations of the Christian marketplace and by the cold, hard politics of the record business. With a deep understanding of just how hard it is for a musician to succeed, he decided to form his own record company, a company where he could do things differently. Squint Entertainment is Steve's ultimate act of rebellion, the hacksaw with which he aims to cut through corporate shackles. The fact that he's operating under the umbrella of the Gaylord Corporation is intriguing, to say the least. If his enterprise works, it could help change the focus of Christian music companies. So far, it's worked pretty well.

Squint has scored that rarest of coups—a hit pop single from Nashville-based group Sixpence None the Richer. As I write this, the group's single "Kiss Me" is sitting in the Top Five of Billboard's Pop Singles chart at hit #2, while its eponymously titled album has shipped over 400,000 units. The video of "Kiss Me," shot by Taylor for $50,000, a mere fraction of a normal rock video budget, has received significant airplay on VH1. The song was even used at Prince Edward's wedding, giving them a worldwide audience of more than one million viewers.

Taylor has had additional successes. The Insyders' Squint *Skaleluia* is the only CD to hit Number 1 on both Soundscan's Rock/Alternative chart and its Praise and Worship chart. Burlap to Cashmere, another Squint group, peaked at Number 10 on the Soundscan Christian music sales chart. Both groups' albums have sold nearly 100,000 units. Steve's next big project is Chevelle, a Detroit rock trio inspired by such heavy alternative rock bands as Tool and Nirvana.

During a year at Biola College (now University) in Southern California, Steve found himself starting to question his beliefs. He worked through his crisis of faith, but the embers of that internal debate still flare occasionally. Indeed, it's clear that this willingness to confront his own values has informed everything he's done in the years since. In the end, it has made his dedication as a Christian artist all the more compelling to his listeners, be they Christian or not.

Like many other college students of his era, Steve was drawn to punk and new wave music. He has said, "The Clash were far and away the biggest influence. I really liked the fact that when they got together they couldn't really play their instruments. I was a music major, and I was pretty good at composition and theory, but I was having the hardest time passing piano proficiency. And then there were the lyrics. They were great with the turn of a phrase, and they were so passionate about what they were singing."

But Taylor wasn't just inspired by bands like The Clash. He was challenged by them. "What was interesting was that The Clash and Sex Pistols were great at pointing out all the problems of the world, but they were short on solutions. So I figured, 'Well, if I'm a Christian, I think I know absolute Truth. Why would I not want to write songs with that same kind of conviction, and yet offer some hope?'"

After a year, Steve transferred to the University of Colorado, which had a fledgling film department. He learned some basic technical skills and made a couple of earnest if uneven films, including one based on a true story where a couple tried to trade their baby for a car. Ultimately, he would recognize both music and film as callings.

In the early 1980s, Christian music simply wasn't prepared for Steve Taylor. Much of the genre consisted of what current Gospel Music Association (GMA) president Frank Breeden called "Sunday school lessons set to music." If country music needed Waylon Jennings and Willie Nelson to help make it hip for hippies, Christian music surely needed Steve to help make it speak to new wavers and modern rockers.

He began recording demos and peddling them in Los Angeles. "I thought it was ironic," Steve said. "The mainstream labels, when I was able to get in, said, 'Your music is interesting, but your lyrics would offend our listeners.' The Christian labels said, 'We don't like your music, and your lyrics would offend our listeners.' The future didn't look very bright."

Steve went back to Denver and kept at it. In 1982, he was invited to perform at the annual Christian Artists Retreat, a Christian music confab in Estes Park, Colorado. Taylor cobbled together a band from the studio musicians who had played on his demo. Thanks in part to his song "I Want to Be a Clone," an indictment of Christian conformity that received a standing ovation, his first real gig was a runaway success.

Sparrow Records founder and then-president Billy Ray Hearn was one of the people in the audience. "He was awesome," Hearn remembers. "He was so fresh— different from anything I'd ever seen." More important, though, Hearn asserts, "I knew he was the kind of person I would like to have on the label. The quality of him as a Christian and as a person was to me as good as his talent."

That didn't mean the music would be an easy sell. "He's a creative genius," Hearn said, but he was so far out of the mainstream of what Christian music was that I wasn't sure we could sell a full album of him. So we did a six-song EP. That thing sold like hotcakes."

Fans of Steve Taylor say that he has always made really great music. But looking back over his career, it's clear that his creative growth has been remarkable. That first EP, *I Want to Be a Clone,* was a modest debut to be sure, recorded in only nine days for a mere $7,000. It was musically tentative in spots, but it was clearly the work of a compelling new voice. Reaction was immediate.

When Sparrow followed that up with a full-length LP, *Meltdown,* Taylor was off and running. He quickly established himself as a manic, almost spastic performer, as interesting visually as he was musically. His shows were "kind of half a play and half rock band," remembers drummer Cactus Moser. "It was fairly courageous in the face of the rest of the Christian music business. He was just too much for some places. There would occasionally be people in the lobbies picketing or praying. They just thought it was too bizarre. It wasn't like a gospel quartet. It was like David Bowie."

He became a favorite on the campuses of Christian colleges and universities. *Meltdown* sold more than 150,000 copies, a terrific figure for the genre. With each successive record, Taylor continued to build an audience and expand his own capabilities as a songwriter and musician.

In the process, he became a key player in bringing Christian music, sometimes kicking and screaming, into the modern musical world and the modern marketplace. It's not always a comfortable role. Amy Grant sold millions of records and hit the top of the charts, while gaining more fans than she lost. "She was very pop-oriented, and her records were aimed at the general market," Billy Ray Hearn observes. "She wasn't breaking new ground musically. And she's a very lovely person. You take a weird guy like Taylor—all the bones and skin—and you've got to have something different going for you."

Gaylord Entertainment, the Oklahoma-based corporation which owns the Opryland Hotel, Nashville's Wildhorse Saloon, and Opry Mills (Nashville's new world-class shopping mall), got into the music business through its purchase of the Opry-related businesses. The firm bought Word Music, one of Christian music's biggest labels, in 1997, and it also owns Myrrh Records, which is a division of Word. It was one of several entities Steve Taylor approached with his idea for a music and film company.

Steve had the support of Jim Chaffee, the head of Myrrh; Loren Balman, the head of Word; and Roland Lundy, the COO of Idea Entertainment, the umbrella under which Squint and Word both function. Even though record sales have been down overall in the last couple of years, it wasn't a bad time to go looking for money. Sales of Christian music have been rising 20 percent every year for the last decade.

In many ways, Steve Taylor is the perfect person to run a label. He brings to Squint much more than his experience as a recording artist. During his time at other recording labels, he worked on a lot of outside projects, both as a record producer and as a video producer. His production of the Newsboys helped turn the young Australian group into a real force and further cemented Taylor's role as someone eager to expand Christian music's sensibilities. And even if he avers that he has no business sense, it's clear that he is used to working within tight budgets. "I'm a really big believer that too much money kills creativity," Steve says, "although I'd like to find out some time."

When he entered negotiations with Gaylord, Taylor wanted to make sure that he would have the elbowroom needed to run a business. "In a lot of the meetings," he says, "I would almost lead with the hardest part, painting the worst picture possible just to see what they were made of. It was going to be expensive and risky, and the model was going to be different. I also said, 'I've been working on this film.' I figured now was as good a time as any, so

I said, 'If you want to do the music, you've got to fund this movie, too.' I was really raising the bar, making it hard for anybody to say yes." But Gaylord said yes anyway.

Taylor decided to call his company Squint after a line from "The Finish Line," one of his songs: "As you squint with the light of the truth in your eyes." He oversees operations from Nashville, and his partner Stephen Pendergast heads up the label's Los Angeles branch.

True to his unassuming nature, Taylor credits his staff with much of the firm's early success. "We've got an extraordinary group of people," he says. "The people on the staff were the heroes on the Sixpence project. And the people at Word and Gaylord were really honorable in sticking this out over the long haul. We were losing a lot of money last year."

Sixpence None the Richer represents a conundrum that has cropped up repeatedly ever since Steve Taylor helped to revolutionize Christian music. Are they, in fact, making Christian music? The members of the group are up-front about their Christianity, but their songs don't blatantly preach the gospel. They are simply a band making the best music they can. Rather than writing lyrics heavy on dogma or pieties, they come at it from the opposite direction—the members of Sixpence draw subject matter from their lives, which are guided and informed by their Christian faith.

For Steve Taylor, Squint is simply trying to put out good music. If you call something Christian, there are so many people who think they know what it is before they ever listen to it. It's why with Sixpence, he just tried to let the music lead. Not long ago, that was a radical notion in Christian music. It's not as radical today, and Steve Taylor is one reason why. He goes into my "Roaring Lambs Hall of Fame."[16]

The Practice Game

I believe strongly that every Christian has at least one spiritual gift. I think this is theologically irrefutable because spiritual gifts are a very well-delineated and defined feature of Scripture. I am not at all sure if it is logical that an entire industry has a spiritual gift. But if this is a defensible way of looking at things, I believe the Gospel Music Association has the wonderful gift of encouragement. The Association exercises that gift in splendid ways by lifting up, encouraging, and inspiring the body of Christ. I am thankful for the Gospel Music Association.

But as a fan and admirer, I want more. As a fellow believer in Jesus, I want more. What Jesus commands us to do has ultimate importance. When we think of who Jesus is, why he came, the work he did on the cross, and the reality of eternity, I think it compels us to do more. How can we do more?

First, I can't find in Scripture anything that says that because we have talent or a gift, even a very special talent or gift, that this relieves us of the universal commands to go out into the world and make disciples. Without question, we are to exercise our spiritual gifts. We are to build up and serve the body of Christ, the church. But even after doing this, we're only halfway down the road that leads to obedience, which brings such joy and gladness.

In some small corners of the church, principally in my own denomination, I have some celebrity because I am a token Christian who has seen success in the field of television. Big deal. The only times I really come close to being engaged, really being involved in the work of God's kingdom, are those rare occasions when I'm able to put something up on the screen which shows him high and lifted up. All the rest is just practice. It's not the real game.

With all Jesus has done for me, I can't just put another tennis tournament on television or fine-tune camera placement so I can show the Boston Marathon better. I can't just sell the Final Four into another country and feel like I'm really getting anything important done because I'm a Christian in television. I need to show him high and lifted up for all to see.

People who work in Christian music have the very same imperatives. They do a great job of lifting up Jesus for fellow Christians to see. This is important. We need to worship Christ, to be inspired by his excellence and his magnificence. But we can't fool ourselves into thinking that this is lifting Jesus up for all outside the Christian subculture to see. We can't fool ourselves into thinking that this is being salt and light, that this is fulfilling the Great Commission. Just as praise and worship music is the right response to God, so is obedience, and so is making life choices that reveal we take the Great Commission and the call to be salt and light seriously.

Dallas, Texas, is my hometown. I think Dallas is a microcosm that illustrates clearly just where we are. Dallas has been tremendously blessed by the gospel. There are historically significant churches in the city of Dallas, as well as the new dynamic Bible-believing megachurches. Two world-class evangelical theological seminaries are in the area. Almost all of the large church organizations have a strong presence in the city. There is a strong Christian newspaper published in Dallas, and there are great and powerful twenty-four-hour Christian radio stations in the market. In many ways, Dallas is a sort of religious Mecca. Much of Christian concern goes on there. There is much coming and going among the people of God. This is one side of Dallas.

The other side is that Dallas is often the murder capital of America. It is also the divorce capital of the country. It leads the nation in the number of topless bars. Abortion is rampant in my city. Race relations are at least as bad in Dallas as in any other major city in the United States. Dallas's schools are infested with drugs, crime, and violence. Some of the biggest savings and loan scandals were perpetrated in the Dallas area, and some people from my own neighborhood went to jail for their involvement. How do we as Christians reconcile these two vastly different pictures of Dallas?

Dallas is also a Christian music center. Christian concerts happen on a regular basis at major churches and elsewhere all around the city. People in Dallas buy Christian records in greater number than perhaps any other American city, and the Christian radio stations large and small send out great sounds twenty-four hours a day. All this is good to a certain extent, but unfortunately the real life of the city goes on largely untouched by all of this Christian musical activity. Why doesn't the Christian presence in Dallas and in the Dallas musical community make any more of a difference?

It is really not all that mysterious or arcane. There is a lot of spiritual salt in Dallas, but it is rarely let loose from the shaker. This is what troubles me most as I wonder what fruit will come from the current renaissance of praise and worship music that has swept the churches. Will all this musical devotion to God in church gatherings lead to devotion out in the workplace, on the campuses, and in our marriages? Or will it simply be a subgame within a subculture that savvy businesspeople capitalize on and exploit for profit, all under the convenient guise of praise and worship to God? Many of the current praise and worship projects are marketed as music born out of a powerful move of the Holy Spirit. I pray that this is so. But if it is true, then we must remember the words of Jesus, who said, "If anyone loves me, he will obey my teaching. My Father will love him, and we will come to him and make our home with him. . . . All this I have spoken while still with you. But the Counselor, the Holy Spirit, whom the Father will send in my name, will teach you all things and will remind you of everything I have said to you" (John 14:23, 25–26).

With an emphasis on praise and worship music, we can keep falling in love with Jesus over and over again, but if this love and devotion, this worship, do not lead to a grateful response of obedience to the teaching of Jesus, it is mere empty religion. The salt must leave the shaker!

In his *The Embarrassed Believer*, Hugh Hewitt claims there are tens of millions of quiet, ineffective Christians and that they are in the majority in most congregations of the world. He says:

> We see the effects of their [the embarrassed believers'] absence from the larger culture just as vividly as we would see the effects of the withdrawal of oxygen from a crowded room. Look. More that fifty million men, women, and children attend Christian church on a very regular basis. That's a very, very low estimate; and I use this purposefully understated number to emphasize the truth of the argument. If even half of this low number were not Embarrassed Believers, then there would be twenty-five million bold Christians wandering around the country. Do you see the evidence of twenty-five million bold Christians at work in the U.S.? Of course not! The counterargument is implausible. The country could not be—literally, could not be—in the condition it is in if there were that many bold Christians wandering around. Let me put it another way. If there were 2.5 million bold Christians in California, do you suppose the entertainment industry would be the way it is? The movie industry? The record industry? Of course not.[17]

Every Sunday, millions of worshipers in the safety of the sanctuary pray and sing worship and praise songs with sincerity and gusto and then vanish into the larger culture and go silent. The reason? Too often we think that by telling one another over and over about who Jesus is that we're getting the ministry of the Great Commission done. When the great Christian music stars come to Dallas, it's a big event. The Christian subculture is all excited. The Christian radio stations trumpet the excitement. Our Christian newspaper runs big features. And the real life of the city goes on without missing a beat. The non-Christian community doesn't even know it's happening. It's a nonevent for them. Why? Nobody went to where they live and work and told them. As far as being salt and light is concerned, we keep confusing practice with the real game. Praise and worship music is growing at a rate of 20 percent per year; are we making changes to the culture at a rate of 20 percent per year?

The Real Game

When I am being interviewed on a Christian radio station, I consider it just practice. It's not the real game. I'm only in the real game when I am on the big secular stations with the tough cynical host fielding calls from the guy who calls up and says, "I'm sick and tired of you Christian fanatics whining and complaining all the time. Get off my station." When I appear on a Christian television show, such as *The 700 Club* with Pat Robertson, that is not the real game. Pat and I are on the same team. That is only a scrimmage. The real game is on *Larry King Live, The Charlie Rose Show,* or *Booknotes* on C-SPAN.

Let's define the playing field in Dallas and, by extension, any other American city. The game is not the Christian concert in a large church setting; the real game is being played at Reunion Arena, at the Myerson Auditorium, the big downtown performance halls. The real game is not in the Christian newspaper. The real game is in the *Dallas Morning News* where every morning six hundred thousand Dallasites go for their picture of reality, to learn about what's important in their world. As big and as important as some of the Christian radio stations in Dallas are, they do not represent the real game. They are only practice. The real ball game is being played with David Gold, the number one talk show host, over on a secular channel.

We can't leave all our best players on the practice field. We need sometimes to get them into the real game. We can't dwell in the comfort of our great church worship and praise programs. We need sometimes to use that empowerment to reach the lost.

Strategic Thinking

I'm really going to show my naivete now. I wonder if anyone in the Christian music industry thinks and prays tactically before going into a city? Could a conversation remotely like the following ever take place?

"Okay, guys, Dallas is coming up in a few weeks. We know Prestonwood Baptist is going to be sold out. Let's be ready to give those good folks a real blessing, a great spiritual lift. We are going to get increased play on KLTY radio, the Christian bookstores will have new displays of our CDs, and the media is doing big features on the group. We're sure to move a lot of units.

"Now on this trip, we've got to break into the Dallas Morning News *and get a feature interview so we can let the city know who we serve and why we do what we do. And what can we do about being a witness for Jesus on SMU's campus while we're here? Could we visit a city high school? How about hitting a secular radio station?"*

Am I just dreaming that that kind of thinking and planning could go on? I hope not. I hope there are people who are thinking and praying tactically about being salt and light, about lifting the Lord up for all to see. And I hope there are people who are thinking and praying strategically, planning and working on big undertakings designed to make Christ known.

Let me offer a couple of examples of what I'm talking about with strategic thinking. In the world of classical music, there are rarely any surprises. But one surprise did occur a few years ago, when a recording of a new work rocketed across the classical music firmament to become an outstanding and astonishing worldwide hit. This was such a phenomenon that *The New York Times* did a major feature on it. Not surprisingly, they missed the real story. It's a story of strategic thinking and praying.

Gorecki's Third

Seventeen years ago Henryk Gorecki, a Polish composer increasingly concerned about the secularization of Polish society and about the lack of spiritual depth to any new classical compositions, began to pray. He asked God to help him write a new work that would reintroduce God both to Polish society and to classical music. The result of the prayers and the work was Gorecki's *Third Symphony*. Even after he finished the work, nothing much happened. Gorecki had a tough time getting it performed. The Communist authorities continually harassed him, but he kept praying.

After the fall of Communism, Gorecki was able to have his work recorded by the London Symphoneta, with words sung by Diane Upshaw in a clear, pure, soprano voice that even in Polish brought a great spiritual message home to all listeners. It became not only a blockbuster hit in Poland but was a runaway best-seller all around the world.

The three movements of Gorecki's *Third Symphony* all relate to the Holy Cross lament. The second movement features a prayer that was discovered on the walls of Gestapo headquarters. It was dated 1944. For those who enjoy classical music, and for all others who value music for its familiarity and depth of expression, the Gorecki Third is a wonderful piece. Others may relish the Third's denial of totalitarian brutality after a century of failed Communism and its shameless discovery of Christian devotion in the midst of suffering.

Gorecki's work represents strategic working and strategic praying, resulting in worldwide impact.

Ken Wales and *Christy*

There is another good example of Christian strategic thinking. Ironically, it also began seventeen years ago, when a then-young film and television producer acquired a piece of classic American material. His plan was to make a feature film, which would honor God and show Christ high and lifted up for all to see. Ken suffered many setbacks, many rejections, and many frustrations. He kept working and praying. Along the way, God changed his vision from producing a movie to crafting the material into a television series. In order to make any progress with it as a television property, he had to give away almost all of the financial rewards that would normally come to a producer of such a major work. He continued to work and pray. Because he did, *Christy* came to CBS. The result of Ken Wales's fighting and praying and working strategically was that we had the first prime-time television series in a long time that was not against God but for him. The heroic character of faith salts our whole culture.

Ken recently shared with me a nagging fear that Christians are not now preparing the material that goes through the doors that *Christy* has opened. He is afraid that the same thing will happen as happened after *Chariots of Fire*, when no one seemed to be thinking and working and praying strategically on other God-honoring movies. Ken fears there will again be a long dry time when nothing is on the big screen or on the major network television screens that brings salt and light. I hope his fears are groundless. I hope someone is thinking, praying, and working strategically. Perhaps this is true of musical projects that might light up screens or Broadway with the gospel? Again, I hope so.

My Dream for the Gospel Music Association

It is said that some people dream in black and white and that some dream in color. I tend to dream in color television. Most of my dreams are about television programs. Let me share a recurring one that I have.

It's not about a series or even a miniseries, and it's not about a made-for-television movie. It's about one hour of great television. It's an hour that exudes creativity, because those who have created it are in close touch with the Creator of all things. Its production values are unsurpassed because every production element has been examined in the light of the excellence of the Savior. I see the program not on the Family Channel, or Vision, or Acts, or Trinity. I see it on CBS, in primetime with a lead-in from their number one program, *60 Minutes*. Because God's people have planned and executed the most innovative and professional tune-in campaign ever, in my dream I see a huge audience gathered around the television sets of America. They are there to watch this very special one hour of television. And then I see it all billed as a gift, a gift of music from the Gospel Music Association.

As the great stars of gospel music and contemporary Christian music are brilliantly showcased, I hear the lambs of Christ roar, producing the sweetest sound you can imagine. And as I listen to the great music and hear the great gospel, I see Jesus the King, high and lifted up for all to see. Not for only the church to see. But for all to see.

Please dream with me. Think tactically about being salt and light. Think and pray strategically. Let's all work to see the King high and lifted up for all to see. Let's do it for Jesus' sake.

Afterword

By Marty Briner

BOB AND I MET AT A SMALL CHRISTIAN LIBERAL ARTS college in January, 1956—a tall, handsome basketball player from Texas and an unknown transfer student from Pennsylvania. And in this same small midwestern town our life journey ended in June 1999.

During the intervening years, we faced many opportunities and obstacles which enriched and deepened our dependence upon God. There were the career challenges and changes beginning in high schools and moving to Christian colleges, state universities, professional football a domed stadium commission, professional basketball, professional tennis, and finally to television. There were family considerations as our children were born— a special-needs son and two lovely daughters.

The underlying love we had for each other and the commitment to our marriage through the great times, the unexceptional and mundane days, and the difficult experiences were protected by God. We both had praying parents who supported us with their love and willingness to help in many ways.

Through the years Bob's sense of humor and his love of fun and relaxation were just what I needed to balance my more serious and practical personality. Many times he sensed when I needed to get away and provided just the needed escape from family stresses.

As our children grew older and opportunities were available for me to accompany him during business trips, he made me feel so welcome and needed. Traveling to numerous countries and exciting cities, meeting people in foreign places and seeing the respect and admiration for him made me realize repeatedly what a very special person he was. So often I took trips with him, adventures for me but working obligations for him. He made sure that I would sightsee and experience the special attractions of that particular city, and later we would enjoy dinner in the evenings together. And there were days when we could relax and sightsee together—special memories. As we made our way through foreign airports, he would be leading the way, I following. Often in busy terminals people would separate us, but I just kept my eyes on a white head which rose above the crowds. I was never lost.

Our children adored and respected him. While our children were younger, he enjoyed being with them—playing many games and swimming. Since he was gone so frequently, he sent them many letters and postcards and brought home loving and thoughtful gifts from the places he had been. But he especially delighted in just talking with them and inventing word games. All of this time spent with them laid a sound foundation for friendship when they grew older. During the sometimes difficult teen years, we had the normal friction and differences of opinion, but the underlying love and respect endured the strains.

Bob had a great sense of humor. He even made fun of himself, referring to himself as the Tubby Texan. He coined many expressions which our family is still repeating. Now, even when a memory brings tears, this often leads to another memory of a descriptive phrase of his, and our tears turn to chuckles. Unknowingly he prepared us for his absence with his gift of humor. Even during the final few weeks, he was cracking jokes, bringing smiles when we felt more like crying.

Another important aspect of Bob was his generosity in money and gifts but also in time and giving of himself. Giving was a natural and spontaneous part of him, and often I knew nothing about it until a letter or call revealed it. He left doughnuts on our neighbor's porch and on our kitchen table. He had Easter egg hunts in our home for the children and even started a tradition of Labor Day gifts. He delighted in sending floral arrangements as an expression of gratitude for a specific reason or just to show appreciation for friendship.

He was generous to various benevolent organizations and parachurch groups. And he showered gifts on me from lovely clothes which he had chosen with excellent taste to a grand piano to flowers to loving notes. He spoiled me, and I loved it.

Integrity was a core part of his personality. This characteristic was evident from the very beginning of our friendship. And he never wavered from this value. Through the years in many situations he was true to his convictions.

As a wife I never had any doubts about his love and faithfulness. For a number of years he was traveling, both in our country and abroad, and was away almost as much as he was home. His phone calls and letters to me and the children kept his presence in spirit real to us. Because of his frequent absences, having him present was even more special.

Bob had the ability to analyze a situation, identifying its main components and reducing a complex situation to several key points. He could see the total picture clearly. People were drawn to him and at ease with him as they discussed problems, asked advice, or just visited. He was a people lover and relaxed and natural as he interacted; from students to executives to government leaders, he put all at ease. But he could also be uncompromising and unchanging in what he believed was right and the correct way to handle a situation.

After writing his first book, *Roaring Lambs,* he became more and more focused on the message of being salt and light in our world. As he traveled, speaking to conventions, colleges, churches, men's retreats, and other organizations, his basic message was the same. There are three universal imperatives for all believers; these are not choices to make but commands to obey—proclaim the gospel of Jesus Christ, make disciples, be salt. The characteristics of salt are purity, glistening whiteness and pureness, penetration, preservation, and flavor. And always he stressed the joy that comes from being obedient.

During the last ten months of his life he struggled so bravely, seldom complaining about the cancer and all the various and numerous painful treatments. His outreach to friends during this time continued by faxes, E-mail, telephone, and visits. He was at peace with God, accepting whatever was in the future for him.

I am blessed with loving, caring children and grandchildren and many loyal friends. But I miss my gentle giant. Heaven seems much closer and even more inviting. I look forward with great anticipation to joining him again for all eternity.

Notes

1. Mark A. Noll, *The Scandal of the Evangelical Mind* (Grand Rapids: Wm. B. Eerdmans, 1994), 10.

2. C. S. Lewis, *Mere Christianity* (Nashville: Broadman & Holman Publishers, 1996), 119.

3. Al Hunt's *Wall Street Journal* column of August 20, 1998.

4. Os Guinness, *The Call* (Nashville: Word, 1998).

5. Ibid., 222–23.

6. Cal Thomas and Ed Dobson, *Blinded by Might: Can the Religious Right Save America?* (Grand Rapids: Zondervan, 1999).

7. Quentin J. Schultze, *Redeeming Television* (Downers Grove: InterVarsity Press, 1992).

8. Bob Briner, *Roaring Lambs* (Grand Rapids: Zondervan, 1993).

9. See my *Deadly Detours* (Grand Rapids: Zondervan, 1996).

10. The Amy Foundation's Church Writing Group

Movement is the very best source for help and instruction. With Christians across the country looking for meaningful areas of service and real ways to be obedient to the "salt" admonition, it is difficult to understand why every church does not have an active Church Writing Group Movement, or something like it.

11. *Deadly Detours* (Grand Rapids: Zondervan, 1996).

12. Ibid.

13. All the emphases in the letter are Dr. Halverson's.

14. Charlie Peacock, *At the Crossroads: An Insider's Look at the Past, Present, and Future of Contemporary Christian Music* (Nashville: Broadman & Holman, 1999), 85–86.

15. Ibid.; and, Harold Best, *Music Through the Eyes of Faith* (San Francisco: HarperCollins, 1993). Also, Harold Best's article on music and worship in the American Gospel Music Academy's music curriculum is a very valuable source of cogent and biblically sound insights. See Harold Best, "Church Music Curriculum," Proceedings of the Fifty-Seventh Annual Meeting, National Association of Schools of Music (Dallas, Texas, 1982).

16. You can read more of Steve Taylor and other musicians who minister outside the Christian ghetto and engage the world of rock music. A very interesting book on this is Mark Joseph's *The Rock & Roll Rebellion* (Nashville: Broadman & Holman Publishers, 1999). The material on Steve Taylor in this chapter was largely taken from an article by Rob Simbeck, "Would You Trust This Man with a Record Company?" in *Nashville Scene, 22 April 1999*, pp. 21–28; used by permission of the author.

17. Hugh Hewitt, *The Embarrassed Believer* (Nashville: Word, 1996), 41–42.

BOB BRINER
August 28, 1935–June 18, 1999

Bob with his father in Dallas, 1938

*With mother in
downtown Dallas, 1940*

Dallas, 1952

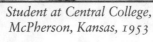

Student at Central College,
McPherson, Kansas, 1953

Junior-Senior Banquet,
Greenville College, 1956

Graduation from
Greenville College, 1956

*Wedding of Robert A. Briner
and Martha Ann Jacobs
in Oil City, Pennsylvania,
August 1957*

*Teacher-coach in
Burns, Kansas, 1957–58*

*Holding son Robby
in Flint, Michigan,
1959*

*With parents in
Canton, Ohio,
1961*

Head coach of Spring Arbor College Bluejays, before taking to the basketball court, 1963–64

Trophy catch, with father in Texas, 1969

General manager of pro basketball team, Dallas Chaparrels, 1971–73

With Clayton Moore, the Lone Ranger, for promotion of Dallas Chaparrels, about 1972

*Children
Rob, Leigh, and Lynn,
1972*

*With Jack
Kramer and
Pierre
Darmon at
tennis
meetings in
Bermuda,
about 1976*

*Acceptance speech when awarded
doctorate of humane letters at
Greenville College, 1977*

*In Shanghai during a trip to
China, 1979. Bob arranged
an ATP-sponsored tour of
the U.S. by a group of
Chinese junior players, the
first in twenty-one years.*

Robert A. Briner, President, ProServ Television, 1980–96

With partner Donald Dell on the set of Sports Probe, which was on the USA Network, 1980

With Stan Smith and Donald Dell at Washington Area Tennis Patrons Service Award Luncheon, December 1980

With ProServ partner Donald Dell, holding NCTA Ace Award for USA Network program Sports Probe, 1981

*In Moscow
about 1981*

*Recipient of the American Baseball Coaches Association Honor Award.
Left to right: Rick Parr, David Altopp, Doug Tkachuk, Marty Briner, Bob
Briner, Dennis Spencer, Ken Trager, and Bob Smith.
January 1984, Dallas, Texas.*

*With daughter
Leigh at
Waterfall
Resort in
Alaska, 1984*

With Brian Polivka in 1984, receiving Freedom Foundation at Valley Forge Award for writing script for A Hard Road to Glory

Fishing in the high Arctic, Baffin Island, July 1985

Briner family at daughter Leigh's wedding to Kevin Ganton, March 1986, in Garland, Texas

With Arthur Ashe, author of A Hard Road to Glory, *holding their Emmys, 1986*

*Accepting the 1986
Sports Emmy Award,
Outstanding Individual
Achievement in Writing,
for* A Hard Road to Glory
TV special

*Working in
the home
office in
Texas, about
1986*

*Easter 1986.
At home in
Dallas*

Fishing off the Baja California Peninsula, Mexico, 1987

With first grandchild, Bobby Ganton, at Central College, McPherson, Kansas, 1988

Receiving Recognition Award at 1991 International Conference on Sports Business, Department of Sport Administration, University of South Carolina

Premiere of the film Dravecky: A Story of Courage and Grace *at Sloan-Kettering Cancer Center, New York City, 1991. Produced by ProServe, the film won the 1992 Best Evangelical Film from Christian Visual Media International. Left to right: Donald Dell, Dr. Robert Smith, Dave Dravecky, and Bob.*

With family at Central College, McPherson, Kansas, 1991

With family when inducted into Greenville College Hall of Fame, 1991

At Greenville College, 1992, with daughter Lynn, who was a senior at the college

*With Edwin and Eileen Pope at the dedication of the Eileen Pope
Photography Lab, Greenville College, 1992*

*Fishing in
Venezuela for
peacock bass,
1992*

*At book
signing
in the
home of
Dennis
and
Jana
Spencer,
March
1993*

*On cruise of
Baltic Sea
countries,
July 1993*

*Christmas 1993. Front: Todd Ganton, son Rob, Reid Ganton.
Middle: Bob, Marty, Bobby Ganton. Standing: daughter Lynn, son-in-law
Kevin Ganton, daughter Leigh Ganton*

*Marty,
Bob, and
son-in-law
Kevin in
Nashville,
1997*

Bob and Barry Landis in 1997 near the Continental Divide outside Estes Park, Colorado, where Bob was a frequent speaking guest

With grandson Todd Ganton at Estes Park, Colorado, 1997

With grandson Bobby Ganton in Spring Arbor, Michigan, 1997

With grandsons Bobby, Todd, and Reid, Christmas 1997

Marty and Bob with grandson Reid, March 1999

Home in Greenville, Illinois, with daughter Lynn, March 1999

With grandsons Bobby and Reid, March 1999

Home in Greenville with daughter Leigh, early May 1999